HOW TO BOARD UP YOUR KITCHEN

AND COOK FROM A HAMMOCK

By Virginia B. Elliott

TOP OF THE MOUNTAIN PUBLISHING
Largo, Florida 34643-5117 U.S.A.

Top Of The Mountain Publishing
P.O. BOX 2244
Pinellas Park, Florida 34643-5117
SAN 287-590X
FAX (813) 536-3681
PHONE (813) 530-0110

Library of Congress Cataloging in Publication Data
Elliott, Virginia B., 1919-
How To Board Up Your Kitchen And Cook From A Hammock/by Virginia B. Elliott.
p. cm.
Includes index.
ISBN 1-56087-042-7: $14.95
1. Cookery.   I. Title.
TX652.E376   1994
641.5--dc20   94-5707 CIP

Manufactured in the United States

Table of Contents

Why You Need This Book

 The older I get, the more I hear my contemporaries say they just wish they could "board up the kitchen." Even our adult children, who are mostly two-career families, say they don't have time for lavish entertaining, or picnicing with a blue-ribbon lunch.

Incidentally, I have a friend who actually did board up her kitchen the day after the youngest child left the nest. Honest injun...she just took herself to the lumber yard, bought two 6' x 6" boards and nailed a nice big old pine "X" across the kitchen door.

She was a full-time director of the media centers in a very large school system and her hubby was on the verge of retirement. That was 9 years ago. And they are still enjoying their freedom from shopping and cooking. She runs every morning, he swims and then they meet for breakfast. She is then off to her job and he to his volunteer work with a hospital and the YMCA. They carry fresh fruit and vegetables for lunch wherever they happen to be at noon and enjoy long intimate dinners together in their favorite restaurants; sometimes a fast food takeout, sometimes candlelight, wine and music. They actually spend less on food, both have lost weight and look terrific. Don't you wish you had her courage?

This cookbook is meant especially for fun and freedom. You can enjoy reading it while resting over a cup of coffee or a glass of iced tea, drowsing over it while swaying in a hammock after planting the seeds for a bountiful harvest. It is for the joy of going the usual cookbooks one better by allowing you to add your own personal touches...You won't find gobs of recipes set out in item-by-item format, yet every page is full of food suggestions and ideas you will use to create your own recipes.

I did include some of my family's favorites for you to use. I hope they will bring back some of your own fond food memories and spark your personal gourmet creativity.

I have found that most really good cooks have five-foot shelves of masterful cookbooks. However, most of these neighborhood chefs, whether men or women, brag, "I read cookbooks for fun, but I cook by the seat of my pants."

And you know something? Our ancestors, whether from the hardy middle Europe; romantic France, Spain or Italy; or the exotic Orient, had to cook by the seat of their pants and use whatever the good land and capricious weather produced. One delightful great-grandmother whose own great-grandmother pioneered in the Ohio Territory in the 1800's but grew up in Germany, said, "Really, for centuries, all the world over, what landed on our plates came straight from God's hands. We had to make do and make it good."

That is surely a sage homily for anyone in charge of marketing and cooking, whether for a family or a corporate party. I have had many years of both duties, and rarely ever had household help.

So while this book is about feeding families, friends and clients the main ingredient on every page, is how to put it together economically, as fast as greased lightning and with as little hard labor as possible. I love food. I love people. I love to swing in a hammock with a brand new bestseller, or walk the beach and play tag with the surf. I love to write. This book shares my secrets for having time for it all.

Did you know that cookbook writers get fan mail? It feeds our egos as well as our souls. One retiree who read the manuscript and ordered three books—one for himself, a new daughter-in-law and a young son just out of college—wrote, "...you should have called it, For New Nesters, Empty Nesters, and Folks Sick & Tired of the Nest!" Well, guess that's you. After you purchase the book, go buy yourself a hammock and cook up a storm.

Credit Where Credit is Due

A special thanks goes to my friend Grant who took me picking for bushels and bushels of tomatoes, which were used in recipe testing for our *3 Tomato 4* book. Grant also brought me pecks and pecks of green beans from his own gleanings, as well as enough zucchini (Italian squash) to sink an immigrant ship.

A loving thank you to my husband who taste-tested everything except the martinis with pickled green beans. Yep, you read it right, trust me.

Also, special thanks to my son David for typing, indexing, editing and re-editing the original manuscript. He could find a misplaced comma in a forest fire! To say nothing of *18* teaspoons of pepper instead of ⅛, and for saving my life, sanity, and immortal soul when I 'glitched' the computer and found my tongue wrapping itself around words which Grandmother never taught me.

This book could not have made it from kitchen to printer without all my family and friends who tasted, critiqued, and listened patiently to my nostalgia.

Further, this book could never have matured from its kitchen-table birth to bookstore maturity without the patience and sense of humor of my writing coach, Phyllis Luxum, who encouraged me to find my "voice" and keep it. Also, Dr. Judith Powell deserves a summer in a hammock for a masterful job of final editing.

Maintenance Manual for the Body Sacred

 When you buy any costly piece of mechanical equipment, from cars to egg beaters, you get a manual. You would have to be blind, deaf, dumb, illiterate, and living on an isolated island all your life to not have been exposed to umpteen manuals to keep operating at maximum this mortal piece of flesh in which we live.

Whole five-foot shelves have been written by nutritional experts and medical doctors pertaining to fats, oils, salt, sugar, red meat, and almost everything else known to man that tastes good.

I am not about to pretend to be a guru in this area. Like most of you, I have been raked over the coals by my gastroenterologist, my dentist, my well-meaning friends, my doggone kids and my mirror. I have read every doomsday book published in the last fifty years about what I should and should not eat. So have you, I bet. When it gets right down to it, and believe me I have tried them all, only one simple rule works for my family. I call it **EUMA:**
EXPOSURE TO FACTS,
UNDERSTAND THE FACTS,
MEMORIZE THE FACTS,
APPLY THE FACTS.

In plain English: read labels, learn the various nutritional values of foods, and cook and eat accordingly. My cooking "bibles" are: *The Nutritional Almanac*, by Nutrition Search, Inc., John D. Kirschmann, Director; *The 8-Week Cholesterol Cure*, by Robert E. Kowalski. The one I really cook and eat by when my husband and I have broken all the rules and need to get serious about our health is *The Pritikin Program for Diet & Exercise* by Nathan Pritikin, the founder and director of the Longevity Center. They are not brand new stars on the publishing horizon, but they really work and have been approved by our family physician. *It is important you never follow special or specific diet plans without first checking with your doctor.*

Healthy Cooking Tips

 Read labels! Remember, pasta is *usually* made without eggs. Noodles *usually* have egg yolks in them. The so-called "Lite" noodles are okay, but we like a more solid noodle because lite noodles slip and slide and get down your throat without ever tasting them. Half the pleasure of food comes from the *process* of chewing. So when the recipe calls for noodles, we use fettuccini or linguini, and brown rice instead of white.

I use a few very simple rules for *healthy* cooking. When a recipe calls for eggs to be incorporated into the ingredients (unless whites and yolks separated), an equal measure of egg substitute works. I find that skim milk with either 1 Table-

13

spoon of butter buds or 2 Table-spoons dry skim milk added per cup, makes a rich tasting substi-tute for fat-rich whole milk.

Buy bottom round on sale and re-move every smidgen of fat. Grind it in your processor and freeze in 8-ounce patties, ready to grill or to defrost and use in rec-ipes calling for ground meat. (Or, use ground turkey.) All recipes are adaptable for vegetarian diets by substitut-ing sautéed tofu for meat.

Many recipes call for cheeses. To cut down on fats, you can use half the amount of regular cheese and half skim-milk cottage cheese. Grate the regular cheese and mix with the cottage cheese. (The pro-cessor comes in handy here.) Also try yogurt instead of sour cream in your favorite dips or toppings. Also, *canola oil is highly recommended by gastroenterologists.*

When you read a recipe or are tempted by a product at the market, remember **EUMA.** Now read, chuckle, cook and in-novate!

Of Taste Buds
and Memories

 Every family in Bloomville, Ohio, during the '20s and '30s had a garden. Believe me, we were *country*— an outhouse, a pump over a spring-fed well, and a rain-fed cistern; no running water in the house. Now that's country! I guess we were poor too. I never realized it until I took my two young sons to visit the area and obtained permission from the present owner to take them through our little old house. It had pie-shaped steps leading up to my room with a low, slanted ceiling under the tin roof. When we climbed into the car and drove away, my ten-year-old said, "Boy, Mom sure was poor." The twelve-year-old quickly said, "Hush up, you dumb-dumb. She doesn't know it."

Nor did we know it at that time growing up in that simple country village. We were always being admonished to take good care of our clothes and toys, so that when we outgrew the use of them, they would still be nice enough to give to the "poor people." We did not give trash to others; it was recycled into scraps for quilts and cleaning cloths. (Grandma even made me many a skirt from the legs of Grandpa's old trousers, but that is another book.) Any food that "wore out" before we could eat it, went to the chickens. Believe you me, we ate well! As I look back, I realize just how frugal Grandma was in the kitchen, but her table groaned with goodies as we did after every bountiful meal.

I don't believe Grandma ever had a cook-book. I certainly never saw her use one. Oh, she and her neighbors would exchange "rules" or "receipts," for who had time to read cookbooks? She just took whatever came from her garden, from the neighbor's generosity, or from off her shelves of canned goods in the basement, and created as she cooked. When it came to measuring she used her hand, or Grandpa's coffee mug, a tablespoon or teaspoon, or her fingers to pinch anything less than a teaspoon.

We had no refrigeration, just the cool basement which was a mud cellar — musty year round, really muddy in the spring, and cold as the heart of a witch in winter. That basement was for serious storage against the long, cold months after harvest and canning.

For daily keeping—a new roast from the market, leftovers or a bottle of milk—all went into a small bucket with its bail tied to a length of rope which was let down into the cavern of the icy, cool well.

So, using up what was ripening faster than we could eat it called for creative measures. Grandma called this *"using it up, wearing it out, making do or doing without."* We did not feel deprived if we had an all-vegetable meal so as not to waste what was at hand. To this day, one of my fondest food memories is a steaming platter of fresh corn on the cob, another platter of thickly sliced tomatoes, onions and green pepper rings, and a loaf of fresh, hot crusty bread. Period. Except, of course, a big bowl of fresh country butter—all you could eat, but no frills or meat. Dessert might be berries from the patch or another slice of bread, spread with butter, brown sugar and cinnamon.

Grandma was an artist when it came to assembling a meatless meal. Picture each plate with a ring of macaroni and cheese surrounding an inner ring of buttered peas and carrots. A whole baked tomato in the middle, all sprinkled with toasted buttered crumbs made from crusts of yesterday's bread. For dessert she would add hot biscuits covered with fruit in season and creamy milk— yummy!

One of Grandpa's favorite suppers was apple dumplings. Let me tell you a good joke on myself. When I was a new bride, my mother-in-law and I were talking food and she mentioned she had not had good apple dumplings since she was a girl. Well, I figured to make brownie points the next time she came to dinner. Using grandmother's old copper luster and tea leaf ironstone soup bowls for dinner plates, I proudly presented a huge pan of steaming apples, each wrapped and baked in a rich pie crust, which filled the air with the aroma of cinnamon and brown sugar. This dish was accompanied by Great Aunt Clara's cut glass pitcher of fresh creamy milk. We sat down and, after grace, a prolonged silence took over.

As I was about to serve Mother Elliott an apple dumpling, she said, "Well, this is different, dessert first."

I nearly died! Apple dumplings and milk always stood alone as the evening meal when I was a child. Good sport that she was, my mother-in-law filled up on my dumplings. She had the good grace to compliment me on my pastry, which wasn't bad, if I do say so as shouldn't; after all, I had watched Grandma mix and roll crust with her light touch for years.

HOW TO BOARD UP YOUR KITCHEN

Those Kitchen-Friendly Italians

 Three vegetables which are easy to grow and are found in the market year round are green beans, zucchini and tomatoes. My *3 Tomato 4* cookbook features tomatoes. Here, we will address green beans and zucchini for dooryard gardeners or city slickers with no yard to speak of.

A careful review of the *Index* will point you in the right direction should you find yourself with a whole bunch of green beans or zucchini on your hands.

Zucchini is one of the several vegetables, popular in dooryard gardens today, which were unknown to the early settlers. According to *Larousse Gastronomique,* zucchini are known as Italian marrows, courgette, courgeron, coucouzelle and zuchetti...as well as plain old Italian squash.

In the garden, zucchini and green beans are two of the most prolific producers, no matter the soil or location. From the earliest harvest, when the little green gourds and slender bean pods are tender and delicate, right up to the final days of harvest when zucchini could be *used as weapons* and green beans become dry and hard, they each provide such a variety of textures and tastes that whole volumes in full color have been devoted to them.

Before you moan, "Oh no! Not another zucchini cookbook!" Bear with me, please. I am absolutely positive you will love this section. It will give you a whole new attitude about these delightful immigrant veggies. So, settle down for a good read and learn some new tricks.

Perhaps like you, I have enough zucchini recipes to paper my kitchen, but I get in a rut and use a couple favorites most of the time.

Well, I had to change my habits and reach back into my memories of Gram when my friend Grant started bringing me enough zucchini to feed an army! Toward the end of the season he was including several huge, overgrown specimens that could have decked a prizefighter with one blow. What in the world do you do with a green summer squash you could use as a baseball bat, whose green skin has become almost leatherlike, and whose innards no longer are firm, juicy nor tender?

I just figured we all love eggplant— parmesan, fried, baked and sautéed— why not try zucchini in these same recipes? Boy, did it ever work. The family liked it better than eggplant, claiming the zucchini produced a dish without the bitter taste often found in eggplant. I also did not have to soak and press the zucchini in saltwater to try to eliminate the bitter taste as you do with eggplant.

However, I think the best experiment of all was the stuffed squash. Okay, I know stuffed zucchini has been around since the first Italian arrived, but these recipes always use young, fresh, tender specimens. Making stuffed squash with overgrown, hard zucchini produces a dish with real taste that you can sink your teeth into.

First I made it with packaged corn-bread stuffing mix and turkey sausage—what raves. Then I tried mushrooms, pecans and packaged traditional white bread stuffing. More raves!

Well, let's get down to business. The following are some recipes which are well worth trying, especially on those zucchini that are still hanging on in the garden and growing like crazy into monsters.

Basic Instructions
for Handling Zucchini

Do for all the stuffed recipes ahead. Scrub well under water and remove any blemishes. Leave stem and blossom ends. Cut very large older squash in half from end to end, making two "boats." You will find that these older, overgrown zucchini have developed very large seeds embedded in a sort of webby, mellow center.

Scoop out and discard this spongy and unappetizing portion, leaving a shell of nice white meat and green skin.

Turkey Sausage Stuffing

Most good butchers prepare their own turkey sausage or at least sell the ground turkey by the pound. It is much lower in fat and cholesterol content than pork or beef, and is very tasty.

Here is a good basic recipe for sausage. Adjust the seasonings to taste.

Turkey Sausage Stuffing

2 lbs. ground turkey meat (if you insist, use pork)

1 Tbsp. dried parsley (or 3 Tbsp. snipped fresh)

1 tsp. dried rubbed sage (some folks double this, but I am not that fond of sage)

1 tsp. salt (more if you like and do not have a sodium problem)

½ tsp. dried hot pepper flakes (You might want to omit this. If so, use 1 tsp. coarse black pepper.)

½ tsp. powdered cumin seed

¼ tsp. each of dried marjoram, basil, thyme

2 cloves of garlic, peeled and minced (in a pinch you can use 1 tsp. garlic powder)

Mix, mix and mix 'til the world looks level. You will need half a pound of the mixture for the stuffed zucchini. You can freeze the rest into patties for breakfast or use again in other recipes calling for sausage. Makes a wonderful addition to spaghetti sauce.

Here is an idea which my men love. *Add about three dashes of liquid smoke or powdered smoke seasoning to the portion you plan to freeze into patties.* Sauté the patties for breakfast to go with pancakes and syrup. The smoke gives it real country taste—better than the greasy stuff from the supermarket.

IMPORTANT CAUTION REGARDING FATTY MEATS: Frozen, high-fat meats should be used in three weeks or less. Sausages go rancid in a hurry even when combined with highly seasoned sauces, and you won't know until you thaw and begin to cook it. By then, all your other ingredients will take on that stale taste and your house will smell awful! Remember to date and label frozen foods. (Ever since I had to dispose of six quarts of sausage-based pasta sauce four hours before a party, and boil cloves and cinnamon to freshen the house, I keep a USE BY DATE list on my freezer door.)

Stuffing For Zucchini Boats

½ pound of the sausage (the butcher's or your mixture)

½ cup finely diced onions

2 cups your favorite packaged bread stuffing, plain or cornbread

Sauté onions and sausage in a non-stick skillet. Mix package stuffing according to box instructions. Add sauteed sausage and onions, mixing well. Mound in zucchini boats. Bake at 350° for 45 minutes in conventional oven; or microwave, covered with wax paper, 7 minutes on high setting. Poke for tenderness and *zap* another minute or two if necessary (remember, you don't want the zucchini to fall apart, or be mushy). ⌐

Regarding Package Stuffings

Leave out butter or margarine, it will taste just as good; or you can sprinkle a teaspoon of artificial butter flavoring into the mix. Be stingy with water too. Your stuffin' should have "body" without being gummy.

Pecan Stuffing

2 cups package dressing

½ cup chopped pecans

½ cup finely chopped mushrooms

Mix per package instructions.
You may also add sauteed sausage and onions (see *Stuffing for Zucchini Boats*).

Parmesan Stuffing

1 cup finely crushed soda crackers
OR 1 cup packaged Italian bread crumbs

1 cup grated parmesan cheese

1 large tomato, peeled, seeded and chopped

2 cloves garlic, finely pressed

l egg plus 2 Tbsp. milk

Mix all ingredients together. It will seem dry, but the tomatoes and mushrooms will release moisture during baking.

NOTE: Also great in mushroom caps — 25 minutes in 350° oven.

Meat Loaf In A Boat

Make your own favorite meat loaf mixture; form it into a stuffing log to fit in zucchini. Smother with sliced onions and green pepper julienne. Bake 45 minutes at 350°. Serve with baked potato and salad.

One very large mature zucchini and one recipe of meat loaf mixture will probably make four servings.

Potato Boats

Prepare zucchini for stuffing. Blanch in boiling water for about 5 minutes. (You want them partially cooked but not mushy.)

NOW, make your favorite mashed potato recipe then heap into the boats. Top with shredded cheese and bake just long enough to melt cheese.

Variations on Cooking Zucchini

We like to mix about ½ cup of sautéed onions into our mashed potatoes. A Jewish friend used to add one raw egg and 3 minced garlic cloves during the mashing, omitting milk, and thereby meeting Jewish dietary law. However, with the present awareness of possible salmonella in barely cooked eggs, this is probably not a good variation.

Try sautéed onions, green peppers and sliced mushrooms topped with crumbled crisp bacon; or shredded ham, cheese, black or green olives.

☞ These same huge veggies are also good washed clean, sliced about ½ inch thick on the slant so they are oval slices. Shake in seasoned flour and gently fry, then proceed to serve as is...*They hold their own flavor.*

☞ Substitute zucchini as the base for lasagna, instead of wide pasta. In parmesan, substitute zucchini for the eggplant.

☞ As platforms for your favorite stir fry mixture, top long sautéed zucchini slices with chopped shrimp, water chestnuts or diced green and red pepper.

Got the idea? Now you be creative and go stuff your own zucchini with something scrumptious!

One of our ritziest hotel dining rooms here in Naples, Florida, serves four delicate, crisply fried oysters on each of four zucchini slices, all arranged on a puddle of Hollandaise sauce. They are a very elegant appetizer with a fancy scallop-cut lemon half on the side, tied up in yellow netting with a green ribbon.

One of my kids took two large left-over fried zucchini slices and piled a package of frozen fried rice on top and cooked it all in the microwave according to the rice package directions. Voilà—an instant lunch or, with soup and salad, a simple dinner.

Shredded zucchini also make wonderful fritters.

Zucchini Fritters

1 cup flour

⅔ cup milk

2 tsp. baking powder

½ tsp. salt

1 egg, beaten

2 cups shredded zucchini

Mix first five ingredients well. Carefully stir in the zucchini and drop by ¼ cup measure into deep hot fat. Watch carefully that they do not get too brown.

NOTE: We are watching cholesterol carefully, so I sauté the fritters on a non-stick griddle with just a smidgen of oil. Use lower heat, watch carefully and turn often.

The nice tender, younger zucchini can stand in for cucumbers, especially if members of your family are sensitive to the gastric discomfort sometimes caused by cucumbers. Sliced thinly and marinated in sour cream dressing; tossed in salads or marinated in vinaigrette, they are a tasty treat.

Sliced longways they make delicious sandwiches on buttered pumpernickel bread.

They can also enhance most any casserole—try it! Here is how:

Enhanced Scalloped Potatoes

For an 8-inch round or square 3-inch-deep casserole you will need about:

2 medium zucchinis

3 medium onions

2 large potatoes

1 rounded Tbsp. Wondra® flour

½ cup skim milk plus ¼ cup dry powdered skim milk

1 tsp. dry artificial butter flavoring

Spray or butter the casserole dish. Thinly slice the zucchini, onions and potatoes. Layer, starting with potatoes, then onions, then zucchini. I salt and pepper meagerly as I layer. Mix Wondra®, skim milk and butter flavoring in a shaker jar. Pour over the vegetables. Bake in 325° oven for about an hour. ⟞

The above is a low-fat version. For a richer dish, maybe for a party, you could drizzle each layer with melted margarine and shredded cheddar or mozzarella cheese and top with buttery, garlic bread crumbs. Either way, the casserole can be assembled ahead of time and baked prior to serving.

Speaking of parties, either young or old zucchini can be used in a ragout. Classic ragouts can be prepared a day ahead and then popped in the oven when the guests arrive, so you can attend your own party. Have a salad waiting in the wings and a store-bought angel cake and ice cream in the fridge.

Zucchini Ragout

2 Tbsp. butter or margarine

1 Tbsp. canola oil

2 medium onions, peeled and diced

3 large cloves garlic, peeled and pressed

2 lbs. zucchini, sliced (peel and seed if mature)

1 lb. fresh tomatoes; skinned, seeded and chopped

Salt and pepper to family taste, but don't smother the fresh flavor of the main ingredients.

1 cup chopped pre-cooked shrimp

1 cup chopped cooked ham

1 cup chopped cooked chicken (use up leftovers)

Melt butter with oil in heavy skillet or flame-proof casserole. Add onions and garlic, cook gently until soft. Add sliced zucchini and tomatoes. Cook over low heat about 20 minutes.

NOTE: *If using old, tough zucchini, cook about 30 minutes.*

At this point you can place it all in the serving casserole and chill overnight for the party the next day.

An hour before serving time, stir in the shrimp, ham and chicken; top with 2 cups shredded mozzarella cheese and bake at 350° for 45 minutes. Enhance with chopped parsley. Serve in wide soup bowls.

It is imperative that you serve a hot, crispy loaf of Italian, French or Cuban bread alongside—for sopping up the juices and melted cheese! If you serve a scrumptious dessert, preferably with lots of fresh fruits, a salad is not even needed to make a great party meal.

For those big old monster zucchinis, you can also peel, scrape out seeds, then slice into half-moon chunks about ½-inch thick; sauté in margarine and serve as a side veggie. Pass the salt and pepper. Remember, they take longer to become tender than younger specimens, but you don't want them mushy. Toss a bit of lemon juice over them at the last minute, and a sprinkle of grated parmesan cheese won't hurt, either.

Try steaming two cups of these zucchini chunks, chill them, and add to any tossed salad.

These zucchini chunks are a delicious addition to stir-fry recipes. The seeded squash can be cut into quarters lengthwise and then in two or three 1-inch fingers. Dip in your favorite batter and deep fry as an appetizer. No, you don't need to peel them, but you can if you prefer.

Try these mellow old things julienned and substitute for French cut green beans in that classic old-timer which we grew up knowing as *Green Beans Supreme*... green beans with French fried onions and mushroom soup. Remember, like your Mama used to make. You never heard of it! *Land o' goshen, child!* Well here it is.

Green Beans Supreme

2 cups canned or fresh green beans (zucchini, yellow squash or broccoli work equally well)

Be sure to thinly cut the vegetable.

Mix with 1 can of cream of mushroom soup, NOT diluted.

Add half a can of French fried onions.

Pile in casserole dish and bake at 325° about half an hour. If using frozen green beans, bake 20 minutes longer.

Try it with mature zucchini, julienned, and bake 45 minutes.

Either way you make it, top casserole with the rest of the can of French fried onions. Bake another 10 minutes.

Tender zucchini can also be used instead of bread for people who are on a yeast-free diet and must carry their lunches to school or work. Split nice fresh young squash in half lengthwise, or slice larger ones ¼ inch thick, lengthwise. Use lunch meat, cheese, lettuce, tomatoes, thinly sliced mushrooms or onions, as fillers. A salad/meat sandwich all in one. You can glue it all together with margarine or cream cheese. All my kids' schoolmates started asking their moms to do likewise. Great picnic fare for dieters, too!

Would you like a wonderful salad for those months of the year when the lettuce is rusty and the tomatoes are so expensive it makes you sick?

Drain a can of green beans—Italian flat, French cut, whole or short cut, as you prefer. Save the juice for soup or drink it as an appetizer. Mix with two fresh young and tender zucchini, julienned.

Dress with your favorite salad dressing or try mine, made from scratch:

Simple Vinaigrette

¼ cup of canola oil

¼ cup fresh lemon juice

1 garlic clove, salt, pepper and paprika to taste

A pinch of tarragon

Put all the ingredients in the blender and whir until it looks creamy. Toss with the green beans and zucchini and chill a couple of hours.

Serve with freshly cut paper-thin onion rings. If there are red bell peppers in your crisper, julienne a few to add color as well as zing.

Top with diced mozzarella or cheddar cheese, salted pecans, or sautéed sliced almonds to make a luncheon entreé. Serve with hot crusty Italian bread, muffins or popovers. ⇐

Well, it seems to me that you ought to have your own imagination buzzing away over the prospect of a bountiful crop of zucchini, young and tender or old and solid. Also seems like we shifted into a green bean harvest. So far, how many new zucchini ideas have occurred to you?

Green Beans Don't Have to be Mundane

 Green beans are not just for boiling with ham and serving up with pot liquor and cornbread any more. You can serve them with equal aplomb in a sterling serving dish, an iron spider, a crockery pot or in martinis. Yes martinis! Read on; or check the index. The world over, beans are a staple in homes from modest cottages to palaces and castles of Europe.

Green beans, when allowed to mature on the vine, whether growing on a bush or climbing a pole, become dried beans for soups, casseroles and ragouts or cassulets. When combined with grains, they provide a perfect protein dish replacing meat for vegetarian and budget meals. Like the Irish potato, beans have fed whole populations in lean times.

Remember, per square feet of garden space, beans can produce more bounty in less time and with less effort than any other crop, except zucchini. More important, beans are threatened by fewer pests and diseases than any other vegetable crop. Even in temperate areas, it is possible to have an ongoing crop from April to late fall by planting every 10 to 14 days. Retirees in high-rise condominiums keep their green thumb exercised growing green beans and tomatoes in balcony pots.

Some climbing beans are even grown for their beauty, such as the scarlet runner, first found in the tropics. It produces a beautiful bright red flower, and edible red and black speckled beans which come on after the showy blooms.

Back in the days of the 1930's Great Depression, high praise for a homemaker was to have her husband say, "My woman can pinch a nickel until the buffalo squeals." Well, Grandma could pinch a penny until the Indian let out a war cry!

My grandmother could wrap a slice of homemade bread around anything that came out of her garden and call it a meal—we call it a canapé. We would never have dreamed of letting one green bean go to waste.

At the market or on the vine, green beans should be very crisp and a lovely fresh green. Like the famous pickles on TV, they should snap and not bend. The smaller the beans are, the more tender they will be and the less time needed to cook.

Let me share a solution to a family problem. Our son is unable to eat high fiber foods because of a serious digestive problem, which omits celery from his diet completely. However, we all love Chinese food...so green beans to the rescue. We *simply use beans in place of celery in all our Chinese cooking.* By using a dash or two of celery salt or chopped celery leaves, we don't miss the celery.

When those wonderful sweet sugar snap peas are in season, I often use them interchangeably with green bean recipes. *As a matter of fact, anything you can do with green beans you can also do with sugar snap peas.*

When the garden yields more green beans than you can shake a skillet at, do just that, get out your skillet and shake it after you have filled it with snapped beans. Before you apply the bottom of the skillet to the fire, add as much fresh chopped celery *tops* as you can scrounge, (remember, flavor without fiber). Shake, rattle and stir until the beans are *al denté*. Serve at once with steak fresh from the grill. If you just have to have a starch, you could throw in a handful of diced cooked potatoes, rice, pasta or a can of garbanzos, but the simple green veggie is just wonderful.

Ask your produce man to save you the green leafy tops he trims off new shipments of celery...before they sell these beautiful tops to the local rabbit farmers. Freeze what you don't use immediately.

Again, a Word about Oils

This bears repeating—our family doctor says canola oil is good for the immune system so I use it, sparingly, whenever the recipe calls for a vegetable oil and in all stir fries, including this green bean recipe.

Grandma would have added about half a pound of diced bacon to her stir fry, but then she lost her gall bladder at age 40!

You could duplicate that lovely country taste of smoked bacon by using diced turkey ham, pork ham or a dash of smoke salt. Did your Grandma add chopped onions? Mine did, when there was one handy. Try it, along with the smoked salt when Uncle Parley from West Virginia visits. He won't even complain that the beans aren't done! You know how us country-types always loved our beans cooked to a limp noodle stage—well you can do that too, but learning to appreciate the wonderful fresh, zippy taste of vegetables cooked to a crisp instead of a "limp" is worth the try and you get twice as many vitamins.

Green Bean Slaw

When your green bean poles are bowing down, make a slaw. Yes, a nice crisp slaw.

If you have a food processor, put 2 lbs. fresh, cleaned beans through the shredder blade. You should have about 3 cups, shredded.

If you don't have a processor, then sliver them with a sharp knife or a potato peeler (Would you believe, some specialty shops even sell green bean frenchers!).

Stir fry them (the beans, not the gadget) in a non-stick skillet with one slice of bacon, diced (Go on, one little ole slice of bacon won't kill you).

When the beans are still very crisp but not raw, drain off the bacon fat completely.

Put beans in a bowl with one thinly sliced onion (about half a cup) and treat with your favorite slaw dressing.

Simple Slaw Dressings #1

1 cup plain yogurt

2 Tbsp. lemon juice or wine vinegar

1 package of Hidden Valley Ranch Dressing® mix

Toss with the beans and chill. Serve in pretty sauce dishes or piled on lettuce leaves. ◁━

Simple Slaw Dressings #1

3 Tbsp. kosher dill pickle juice from a jar of pickles you bought at the store, or your own. (See the easy kosher dill pickle recipe in my *3 Tomato 4* book.)

½ cup cholesterol-free mayonnaise.

Mix well. Toss with beans. Chill and serve. ◁━

You can gussie up any kind of slaw or salad with strips of sliced pimento or slices of stuffed olives.

Do you remember that wonderful *Wilted Salad* your grandmother used to make with dandelion greens? If you don't, you were a deprived child, because once tasting it, you could never forget it (see *Chapter Fourteen*). Well, you can do the same thing with that bountiful crop of green beans from your garden.

Wilted Green Beans

1 lb. young, tender beans, stem and string them (or you may use canned or frozen beans)

8 or 9 green onions, green part and all, chopped

3 cups chopped chicory (endive) cut 2 inches long

Now, sauteé the green beans and onions in a non-stick skillet with about 2 Tbsp. broth from your freezer, or boullion crystals.

When beans and onions are *al denté*, add ¼ cup red wine vinegar and ¼ cup good olive or canola oil to the skillet, salt and pepper to taste. Add a dash of sugar to cut the vinegar.

Bring to a boil. Pour over and toss with the endive. Serve hot in bowls with fresh hot bread for soppin' up the dressing. ⟻

NOTE: I mention dry Ranch-type dressing mix often and you might like to know that you can purchase it in the large restaurant size (26 ounces) under the Tone's® label, at warehouse depots such as *Sam's Club*. I use it for all kinds of seasonings, not just salad dressing. *Mix a rounded Tablespoonful into a cup of flour for dredging chicken to fry*; it rivals the Colonel's®, I kid you not!

Green Bean Fritters

We all have tried creamed green beans, boiled beans with butter, green beans vinaigrette and beans in soups. But slivered beans also make great fritters, using the same procedure as for zucchini fritters. (see *Index*)

Sometimes you want a really filling and spectacular casserole to accompany a barbecue, a roast or a seafood entrée. The following concoction can be doubled or tripled and put together a day ahead of time.

This will feed 4 as the one main accompaniment to a meat entrée or 8 as a side dish. Go from there, doubling as your guest count mounts.

Aunt Clara's
Scrumptious Beans

Use either 1 can cut green beans, or
1 10-ounce box frozen beans, or
¾ lb. fresh green beans

Now, slice up enough onions to make 2 cups

4 ribs of celery, thinly sliced on the slant to make about 2 cups

1 large bright red pepper, sliced julienne

1 can of garbanzo beans, do NOT drain

1 half pound plastic container of pimento cheddar cheese spread from the deli section

½ cup flavored bread crumbs for thickening

½ cup milk

Mix everything together in your prettiest casserole dish. Bake 45 minutes at 350°. Top with half a cup of salted sunflower seeds (pepitas).

If using fresh beans, snap and string them by pinching off stems and pulling down "seams." Cut into 1-inch lengths.

NOTE: If using canned, drain the juice and save it for soup or drink it instead of a martini.

TIP: Flavor and nutrition trick: mix the juice from the can of green beans with ¼ cup dry skim milk. Use in recipes instead of milk.

Serve with pride and sell the recipe! If the kids ate all the sunflower seeds during last night's movie, slivered almonds will also do nicely.

One of my best friends did me one better when I gave her the recipe. She topped her casserole with salted pecan halves and chopped chives. The combination was just heavenly. It took real restraint not to be jealous! Now it's your turn to out-do us both...and raisins won't do!

Do you stand there at the kitchen sink, gulping a few spoonfuls of leftover green beans instead of feeding them to the disposal? Shame on you.

Put them in a small half-pound margarine tub for the freezer to add later in soups, omelets, casseroles. Yes, I said omelets. Green beans really are delicious scrambled into fresh eggs or egg substitutes and folded into omelets. If you add a handful of seasoned croutons to the omelet, you have what the fancy Italian chefs call a *frittata* and what my Grandmother just called *scraps and eggs*.

Any leftover vegetable you can name, along with a handful of croutons or snipped up crusts of bread, mixed with eggs, will make a wonderful supper if you serve it with a salad. Call it a frittata if you must, but Grandma would snort.

My grandfather would eat anything between two slices of bread. But the one thing he invented that we all liked is the green bean sandwich. Don't gasp.

Our favorite version is to pile leftover plain, boiled or steamed green beans on seeded rye bread, thickly buttered, and add very thinly sliced sweet onion and plenty of salt and pepper. As a midnight snack it could lead to romance, onions and all!

This little family story reminds me to tell you of one of my most well received canapés. Remember your mother's delicate little cucumber sandwiches with the crusts cut off? And her tender white bread rolled around asparagus stalks? Well, try this on the bridge club or that reception you offered to host.

Green Bean Canapé

Cut the crusts off fresh whole wheat bread slices. Spread them with softened cream cheese which you have mixed with 2 Tablespoons of finely chopped chives.

Roll each slice around three or four very young and tender steamed (*al denté*) green beans. Fasten with toothpicks and chill at least an hour. Canned whole green beans, well-drained, or frozen whole beans steamed *al denté* can be used. Fresh is best! ⟜

I sometimes use pickled okra, raw Chinese pea pods, raw sugar snap peas, or canned whole baby corn this same way. Thin-sliced seeded rye bread and butter instead of chive cream cheese really complements the corn.

Alternative Salads

We did mention one or two alternative salads back a few pages. But here in South Florida, we have times when the lettuce is all rusty, and the imported Mexican tomatoes are expensive and contaminated with insecticides. Here are some ways to satisfy that taste for a savory salad without paying four dollars a pound for Belgian endive or resorting to an old standby—three bean salad. Not that three bean salad is anything to sneeze at, but it is not exactly earth-shattering, now is it?

When preparing salads, an old Spanish proverb will serve you well: "...A miser with vinegar, a spendthrift with oil, a wiseman for salt and a madcap to toss like crazy."

TIP: When draining canned vegetables, always freeze liquid in margarine tubs for soup stocks or meat sauces. Be sure to label them.

Salad From Cans

1 can artichoke hearts in water, drained

1 can hearts of palm in water, drained

1 can whole Italian plum tomatoes, drained (poke hole in each tomato and drain)

Place in your prettiest glass dish and pour ½ cup of your favorite vinaigrette dressing over it. You can add red onion rings too. Let season for at least an hour in the fridge. Provide a slotted spoon and serve in glass sauce dishes.

P.S. You can add any of the rolled canapé vegetables mentioned on the previous pages if you like, for a perfect salad to offer at a one-plate, one-utensil buffet.

Edible Christmas Buffet Centerpiece

Steam to *al denté* stage the best florets of 2 large heads of broccoli. Chill at once in ice water. Arrange wreath-style on a large, white platter.

1 can of well-drained pimentos, julienne. Use these red strips to create a "garland" over the broccoli.

Center the platter with a pretty compote filled with cherry tomatoes or large red radishes. Serve your favorite dressing on the side.

OR arrange slices of cherry tomatoes and large radishes on wreath and put dressing in middle. ⟜

Rice Salad
(A Luncheon Entree
or Great with Barbecue)

2 cups cooked rice, chilled

2 cups cooked fresh or canned cut green beans, drained and chilled

1 cup each small dice celery, green pepper, red pepper, green onion

½ cup sliced ripe pitted olives

TIP: We love those briny Greek olives but they do not come seedless. So use an old-fashioned cherry pitter or the tip of a potato peeler and the seeds will pop right out.

1 cup honey roasted pecans, or smoky almonds, *according to your taste. NOT BOTH.*

½ cup real mayonnaise mixed with 1 Tbsp. each fresh lemon juice and orange juice.

Toss all together and chill. This will feed about 8 or 10 and can be done ahead of time. (Don't you just hate to be in the kitchen during your parties?)

YOU WILL NOTICE I RARELY MEN-
TION THE ADDITION 0F SALT OR
PEPPER. *We simply do not add either
when cooking fresh vegetables, since we
are all trying to learn to appreciate the
true flavor of foods and to cut down on
sodium intake. Pass lemon wedges instead.*

Pickled Green Beans

1 lb. tender whole green beans. Steam or microwave until very *al denté*. Drain at once and
chill in ice water to stop the cooking and preserve the nice fresh color. When you cook green
beans in the microwave, they stay as bright
as the moment they were plucked from the
bush or vine.

Add thinly sliced rings from a large, red Spanish or Vidalia sweet onion. Marinate at least
three hours or overnight in your favorite
vinaigrette dressing. Serve with slotted spoon
or tongs along side any meat, fowl or fish.

Now, About Those Martinis

Just stick a pickled green bean from
the above recipe in a martini, instead of
an olive, and startle your guests. They

will ask for extra beanies in their martinis and talk about it for months and copycat you at their next party. We call it a "beanie-tini." No green beans handy? Try a hot pickled okra.

Canned sliced pickled beets topped with shredded carrots that have been moistened with a bit of slaw dressing also makes a pretty (psychedelic pink) winter salad.

Also, try mixing shredded carrots with crushed pineapple and raisins. Even orange and grapefruit sections served in a compote will suffice as salad in a pinch.

And remember "Candle Salad." Oh come on, you're not *that young!* Well, alright then, I'll introduce you to one of my favorite childhood memories—teaching my grandmother something new.

When I was in elementary school (before 1933 and that is all I'm gonna tell you about my age.) the Home Economics classes prepared the school lunches. After all, that school included all 12 grades, and those high school Home Education teachers really taught the girls to cook, and not just white sauce.

One of the most popular items they made and served was candle salad. Here is how to light up any meal.

Candle Salad

In a small flat bottomed sauce dish lay two canned pineapple slices, one atop the other. Dip the rounded end of half a banana into mayonnaise and stick the flat, cut end into the hole in the pineapple stack. Now, top this banana with a maraschino cherry and you have a candle salad.

Grandma was a good student and served it often for company after I showed her how.

Another childhood memory is pickled beets and eggs. They were served at all family reunions, church suppers, Fourth of July picnics and at most any summer lunch or dinner when company was coming.

Pickled Beets and Eggs

1 bunch fresh beets with tops—should have at least 6 beets.

Cut tops off about an inch above the beets. Wash these tops thoroughly under running water and chill in a plastic bag until later. (Recipe coming up)

Scrub beets, leaving root and short stems intact. Bring to boil in water to cover. Simmer on low heat until tender.

Hard-boil 1 dozen eggs while beets are cooking.

Lift beets with slotted spoon and cool. DO NOT DISCARD POT LIQUOR.

TIP: For Perfect Hard-Cooked Eggs: Do not use aluminum pan. Start in cold water to cover, with lid on pan. Bring to boil; lower heat, simmer for twenty minutes. Pour off water. Cover eggs with ice cubes. Add 1 cup of cold water. Let sit for 5 minutes and drain off cold water. Holding lid on tightly, give the pot a couple of good bounces and the shells will practically fall off.
When the beets are cool enough to handle, slip the skins and discard them.

Put whole, shelled eggs into a large glass canister or a large, deep casserole dish with a cover. Slice the beets over the eggs.

Next you make the brine. Bring the beet juice back to a boil and add 2 Tablespoons sugar, 2 Tablespoons pickling spices, and 1 cup of cider vinegar. Simmer away for about 10 minutes.

Pour over the eggs and beets until the container is full and the eggs for sure are covered in brine. Put the container lid on tightly and chill in fridge for at least 24 hours.

Serve in a pretty, white bowl as an added attraction to any meal. ⟣

When you have a couple eggs and a few beets leftover, which is hardly ever...slice them onto a salad plate lined with lettuce or parsley, top with thinly sliced onion rings and some chopped celery leaves. It makes a lovely winter "savory."

Pickled eggs also make beautiful deviled eggs, topped with a tiny slice of sweet gherkin pickle. Picture it...red, yellow and a touch of green.

Now about those beet tops, or greens as Grandma called them. Steam them in a very small amount of water until tender, like cooked spinach. Fry two strips of bacon crisply and crumble. Serve the greens topped with the crumbled bacon. Pass salt, pepper and vinegar at the table. (I am drooling as I write.) They're just as good hot as cold.

Easier, Faster Beets and Eggs

If you are in a hurry, or there are no available fresh beets at market, just boil up some eggs and open 2 cans of sliced pickled beets and dump them in on top of the shelled eggs and chill overnight.

Yesterday, when I was young—congealed salads were the standby of every cook who wanted to make an extra effort for a special meal. I remember I used to wonder why they were called salads, and I still do, when most of them were sweet enough to decay porcelain dentures.

I am proud to say Grandma usually stuck with the savory kind, you know, perfection salad—made with lime gelatin with carrots, cabbage, onions and celery, all diced and shredded to a fair-thee-well. Or canned tomatoes, Knox® Gelatin and whatever kind of vegetable she had handy. Sometimes she would even pop in some chopped leftover ham or chicken.

Well here is one of my own. On second thought, maybe it came from my good buddy Barbara. Anyway, it is mighty good and worth every minute of the time it takes. But it redeems itself because you can make it up to forty-eight hours before serving.

Chicken's In The Garden

2 envelopes Knox® unflavored Gelatin

1 Tbsp. sugar

2 rounded Tbsp. dry ranch-type dressing mix

3½ cups canned or homemade chicken broth, de-fatted, heated to boiling. If using condensed canned broth, be sure to measure after adding water per directions

2 Tbsp. fresh lemon juice

1 cup cut, cooked green beans

1 cup diced celery

½ cup diced green onions

1 cup diced young tender zucchini

1 8-oz. can well drained, sliced water chestnuts

2 cups finely diced cooked chicken meat

NOTE: The gelatin ingredients are slightly varied from those on the Knox® envelope and are doubled. However, make up the gelatin mixture using my ingredients and the box directions. Pour about ¼ inch of gelatin in the bottom of a large ring mold or flat 9"x13" glass dish. Place in freezer until firm. Then, mix all solid ingredients with rest of the gelatin mixture and fill mold or dish. Chill until set. Serve with following dressing on side and pass pepitas (roasted sunflower seeds) to sprinkle over portions. ⌐

This dressing is also delicious to accompany a chilled platter or combination of any steamed vegetables.

Dressing for Congealed Salad

Beat together:
1 cup real mayonnaise

3 Tbsp. fresh lemon or lime juice

Pinch dried tarragon

$\frac{1}{8}$ tsp. nutmeg

Just a dash of Louisiana Hot Sauce (Tabasco®)

Just a dash of dried dill weed ⌐

I'm here to tell you that everyone will want this recipe for concealed salad, It will stand alone as a luncheon entrée or as a cold supper with a platter of sliced tomatoes and cucumbers on the side. A crusty loaf or a pan of biscuits or hot popovers will team up perfectly for hearty eaters. And the beautiful part is that it can be made a day or two ahead, stored in the fridge and ready to serve on your committee meeting days.

I am sure that by now the right side of your brain—the creative side—is bubbling over with new ideas to use up too many green beans, or ways to brighten meal times and parties and to earn yourself applause.

What to Do with Leftover Veggies

Why not try chopped leftover veggies in pancake or waffle batter. Combine with a slice or two of leftover ham, diced and mixed into a can of undiluted cream of chicken soup and serve over waffles, unsweetened French toast, hot biscuits, mashed potatoes, baked potatoes, cornbread—adding some chopped raw onion too. Purée leftover zucchini or green beans in your blender with any cream soup of your choice (actual recipes listed in *Index*). Serve heated or chilled *a la vichyssoise*, dressed up with chives, parsley or watercress.

Purée any cooked vegetables with a glass of tomato juice. Voilà, your own V-8®. Purée fresh or leftover cooked vegetables and add to roast drippings for a rich, tasty low-cal gravy. Add a few crushed, seasoned croutons for thickening instead of flour.

I have purposely not included zucchini muffins and all the usual good recipes easily found in almost any general cookbook, or those books devoted especially to this prolific Italian. Lives there a cook, even in Timbuctu, who has not been given at least one of these glossy little books, in full color yet?

My desire is to turn you on to creating something new on your own—enter a contest, get some applause, have a bunch of fun with your garden or at the produce counter or the country stand on the edge of the fields a mile down the road. If you are fortunate to live in an area where the fields are open for *U-Pickers*, don some comfortable shoes, a hat with a brim and go get some exercise and get acquainted with the taste of food fresh from its source, the good earth.

I bless God and the farmers that I live in an area where I can harvest fresh vegetables without having to plow, fertilize, plant, irrigate and debug fields of crops and pray for more rain, or for less rain.

Even if you are a city-bred high-rise occupant, a trip to these nearby fields will take you back to your Mama's roots, and you will feel so productive when you serve up your "harvest."

You might even try growing an eggplant bush, a couple of tomato plants and a pole of green beans in *terra cotta* pots on your balcony.

A Word About Storage of Fresh Vegetables

Keep the crisper drawers in your fridge scrupulously clean... bacteria grows like weeds even in this cool area. Use those plastic lacy grids in the bottom of the drawers as they allow air circulation under the vegetables. The plastic sponge mats get messy, can harbor bacteria and are a pain to clean.

If you are not going to cook green beans the day you bring them home from the field or market, wash them well and pack into self-sealer plastic bags with a dampened paper towel. Zip them up, leaving plenty of air in the bag. They will still taste fresh off the vine in two or three days... but don't delay use any longer or they will become limp, weary and tasteless. Don't snap the stems and strings until ready to use.

Zucchini should just be wiped off with a damp paper towel to remove any sand or soil, and then washed with a scrub brush when ready to cook.

NOTE: Fresh Italian squash have tender skins and will deteriorate rapidly if handled harshly and stored for any length of time. I like to keep a green Scotch Brite® pad to clean vegetables. It really cleans them nicely and will scrub a carrot in a jiffy—just wrap and twist.

Even at the market, I like to pick my own beans, bean by bean; and asparagus, stalk by stalk; and zucchini squash by squash. I just don't like those pre-selected and sealed packages which are apt to conceal a spot of mold or a wounded vegetable. That's why I really enjoy the *U-Pic* fields when they are available.

If you find yourself carried away in the fields and come home with literally gobs more than you can use before they grow stale, both green beans and zucchini freeze very well.

Just wash zucchini very clean, slice into freezer containers and freeze. Green beans should be washed carefully, and "strung," which means snipping off the stem ends and pulling it down the seam. (I like to freeze them whole so when I decide to cook them, I can serve them whole or cut up—whatever my recipe calls for.) Next, plunge the beans into boiling water for about five minutes and then into ice water to stop the cooking process. Drain well and package tightly together in freezer containers and freeze. I swear by Seal-a-Meal® bags and sealer, as I can control the size of my packaging. What could be easier? And you can be sure you will save dollars over the cost of national brands of frozen vegetables from the freezer case at the supermarket.

Frozen zucchini will not need a very long cooking time and can be done in the microwave in a jiffy. Just be guided by the instructions in the frozen vegetable section of the cookbook that came with your microwave oven. Four minutes on high should be about right for two cups. Then add minutes according to how much you are cooking, better to have to add time than to overcook. So, you see, there really is something new under the zucchini vines and the green bean poles!

But before we leave the garden, let me give you several more alternative salad ideas and ways to serve those veggies.

More Winter Salads

Crunchy Salad

Cut 2 young, tender zucchini into 2" julienne

Cut 2 young carrots into flat curls with your potato peeler

Snap and string ½ lb. fresh tender green beans

Cut 5 sticks of celery into slantwise thin slices

Open and drain a can of sliced water chestnuts

Steam the green beans *al denté*. Toss with all of the above in a bowl with your favorite vinegar and oil dressing. Personally, I like a bottled caesar salad dressing for a change. And a sprinkle of bleu cheese is wonderful over this vegetable medley.

Snappy Fruit Bowl

2 bright red, crispy Delicious® apples

1 green Granny Smith® apple

½ cup each red and green seedless grapes

1 cup celery, small dice

6 oz. raspberry yogurt

1 can diced pineapple, drained, keep juice

1 cup smoky almonds

Polish, core and dice apples, and put in a bowl with a cup of pineapple juice to keep apples from darkening. This much can be made early in the day. When ready to serve, drain the apples, adding the juice to the rest of the pineapple juice for breakfast tomorrow. Toss all but the almonds together in a pretty bowl (or portion into sherbet glasses). Top with almonds. Serves 8 as salad; 4 as a luncheon entreé, with hot popovers or bran muffins.

Get glitzy if you want to decorate with cold kiwi slices or big black sweet cherries when they're in season. ⟢

Way back beyond yesterday, when I was being courted while still in high school in Toledo, Ohio, our dates used to take us to a road house, the Dixie Inn, on the old highway between Toledo and Detroit (we were dating freshmen in college). I still get tingly at the memory of how very grown up and sophisticated we felt, being ushered to a cloth covered table with all kinds of silver on either side of a pewter serving plate (sure did beat the Kewpie Drive-In). When the waiter snapped open the huge snowy linen napkin and placed it on our laps, it almost made us gals swoon. The very idea that way in the back of the building somewhere there was *gambling* going on only added to our thrill. Our parents never learned we had been to dinner at the Dixie Inn until well after we had married the college boys.

The moment you sat down you were served a bowl of crisp celery hearts, tender green onions, black olives and huge stuffed olives, along with a bowl of their famous cottage cheese salad and a basket of hot bread.

Everyone from northwestern Ohio/ southeastern Michigan, whoever ate there, copied it as an appetizer with crackers or as salad mounded on a bed of Bibb lettuce and tomato slices.

Road House Cottage Cheese

Mix together 2 cups of large curd creamy cottage cheese, 1 can of well-drained kidney beans, 2 Tbsp. chopped chives, and about a cup of finely diced garlicky kosher pickle.

Stuffed Egg Salad

Boil enough eggs to serve each person 3 halves.

When eggs are cool, cut in half as for deviled eggs. Mash the yolks with a level teaspoon of plain yogurt for each yolk.

Then, for each egg, add the following:
1 tsp. minced black olives

1 tsp. dill pickle relish

⅛ teaspoon dry Ranch-type salad dressing mix.

Mix thoroughly and pile into whites. Top each with a huge green olive stuffed with an almond.

Arrange three egg halves to a person on a bed of spinach leaves that have been dipped in Caesar salad dressing and drained. This provides protein for a vegetarian meal, or extends a casual Sunday night supper of soup and crusty bread. ⟜

A Super Sandwich: 2 Versions

Here is an easy, tasty, nutritious, quick open-faced sandwich for serving one or a committee. For a group, most of it can be prepared ahead of time. For a luncheon, spiced peaches or apple rings on the plate add color and a sweet touch. A thick slice of fresh ripe tomato with a thin green pepper ring adds a savory.

TIP: You may use low-fat cream cheese and mozzarella; keep the bleu .

Broiled Sandwich for One

One thick slice of French bread, sliced on the slant to give you an oblong "raft."

½ cup each of sliced zucchini and onion rings

1 Tbsp. each of cream cheese and bleu cheese

3 Tbsp. grated mozzarella (or your favorite) cheese.

Sauté zucchini and onions in non-stick skillet until limp. Toast bread on both sides. Pile zucchini and onions on bread. Combine cheeses and pile on top of vegetables. Run under broiler just long enough to melt cheese. Pour yourself a glass of white wine. ⊂—

Broiled Sandwich for Eight

Prepare one slice of bread for each person (see *Broiled Sandwich for One*).

Increase rest of ingredients, times 8.

Have vegetables sautéed and at the ready.

Have the cheeses thoroughly mixed together.

When ready to serve, toast the bread, and proceed same as for one. Salted pecans on top make it special.

Laying out the bread on a cookie sheet to toast on one side, and then assemble and broil, makes it easy and fast. Have the fruit chilled and on the plates, or the tomatoes and green peppers sliced and on the plate. And that's my song—easy and fast! ⊂—

Super Relish

To compliment steaks, burgers, hot dogs, roasted pork or ham.

Shred 3 medium zucchini, 2 medium onions, 1 medium green pepper, 1 medium red pepper, and 1 large or two small tart, crisp, green apples.

Shred, don't pulverize. Lightly toss all together in a bowl.

Now add:
2 Tbsp. each: catsup, dijon mustard and wine vinegar

A pinch each of tumeric, celery seed

Salt, pepper, sugar, sparingly to taste

Makes about a pint. Should chill 24 hours.

What's a cookbook without a good *quick and easy* soup that tastes like you slaved all day over a steaming pot?

For a great lunch or to extend a meal, read on.

Zucchini Soup

1 can cream of chicken soup, diluted with

1 can of milk

1 medium to large zucchini, shredded

1 large clove of garlic, minced

Heat slowly, stirring all the while so it does not stick to the bottom of the pan. (Or microwave in a 2-quart glass measure for 4 minutes on high.) Serve it with garlic croutons floating on top. ⟜

Polk-a-dot Potato Soup

To add a new taste and a bit of color to plain old canned cream of potato soup, chop green beans into very short cuts; sauté in about a Tablespoon of margarine in a 2 qt. pot. Add the canned soup and a can of milk. Serve with Baco Bits® or nutmeg on top. ⟜

TIP: Two-inch chunks of zucchini and whole raw green beans added to a hearty stew about 10 to 15 minutes before the carrots and potatoes are tender, will make it go farther and taste terrific. We add both to a New England boiled dinner.

Coming up—easy picnics, dinner parties and unique breakfasts.

Breakfast for Breakfast-Haters and Moveable Feasts for Picnic-Procrastinators

 Breakfast-haters usually love that morning meal if someone else prepares it for them *and* if there is plenty of leisure time; except kids, of course, who never like anything that is good for them. So why not give them something out of the ordinary that they'll never dream is nutritious? That is what my Grandma did—and it made a breakfast-lover out of *me*.

My own breakfast rebellion probably took root in front of a bowl of yukky, grey cooked oatmeal, swimming in milk that refused to soften the stuff no matter how briskly I stirred. One morning Grandma *whisked a bit of cinnamon, brown sugar and a big lump of freshly churned butter into the oatmeal as she cooked it.* I remember that wonderful aroma, like freshly made butterscotch pudding. The first taste proved as delightful.

I was never a sweet-tooth kid; I preferred salty foods. Given the choice between chocolate cake or another helping of potatoes and gravy, I would always choose the latter.

So, occasionally, Grandma would *vary the oatmeal seasoning by using salt and pepper and her sweet butter.* It was almost as good as grits—if you're from Dixie or a converted Yankee; or soup if you're married to a Canadian (I swear, these north-of-the-border types eat soup for breakfast!)

Soup-er Starters

The first cool day of winter, my new (Canadian) husband astounded me by asking for hot cream of tomato soup for his morning meal. Who ever heard of soup for breakfast?

Well, it warms the cockles of your heart, is nutritional, and can be sipped from a mug while you're reading the morning paper, or even taken in one of those spill-proof insulated mugs to the office if you're running late. Just be sure to make it with milk for added protein and calcium. You can even whir up the can of soup and a can of milk into a pitcher the night before and just heat a mug at a time in the microwave the next morning.

A real palate pleaser, and a quick fix to boot, *is to make a cup of instant-mix cream of chicken soup from the packets sold in boxes and pour it over a handful of seasoned croutons.* It is just as good for breakfast as it is for lunch. A handful of shredded cheese stirred in is even better. You do keep packs of shredded mozzarella and cheddar in the freezer, don't you?

Waffle Sandwiches

Was there ever a school kid or a career mom who didn't oversleep once in a while? *A toasted frozen waffle sandwich spread with sliced banana and peanut butter; or made with lunch meat and Swiss cheese; or cream cheese and dates and walnuts or pecans,* is simply delicious. It is good for you and can be made in a hurry and eaten on the run.

Desserts for Breakfast!

Who says dessert is just for after lunch and dinner? *Try cutting up a baked apple over a scoop of fruit sherbet, vanilla ice cream or leftover pudding from the night before, and sprinkling your favorite cereal over the top.* As a matter of fact, any pudding—rice, bread, vanilla, butterscotch, whatever—is great with cereal topping for crunch and just enough milk added to make it pleasant to eat.

And pie. Yes, pie for breakfast. I drool now at the memory of the day *Grandma finally allowed me to have a slice of warmed apple pie with a slab of cheddar cheese on top for breakfast,* just like Grandpa was having. I tell you, it sticks to the ribs, and no card-carrying breakfast-hater can resist.

I was quite grown up with kids of my own when I discovered fruited low-fat yogurt. I again started to like *cereal, topping it with yogurt instead of milk and sugar.*

Yukky Buns

A brand new breakfast idea was born from necessity one morning when I was out of cereal and eggs *and* frozen waffles or pancakes. It must have been the first day home after vacation or the morning of grocery shopping day.

I did find two frozen hot dog rolls in the freezer. I scooped out a bit of the soft bread, which made each roll sort of like an oblong bread bowl (a grapefruit knife or spoon is handy for scooping).

I buttered them, sprinkled them with cinnamon sugar and toasted them lightly in the toaster oven. Then I let the kids stuff them with their choice of peanut butter, jam and jelly, sliced cheese and lunch meat. They outdid one another in creating their breakfast *Dagwood.* (If you are too young to know what a *Dagwood* is, ask your mother.)

Incidentally, my kids have always called these *yukky buns,* and now make them for their own kids. We nearly lost the first daughter-in-law on that one.

Quick Breakfast Ideas

Have you ever thought of heating up the leftover *rice for breakfast*? Try it with diced ham, green peppers and tomatoes, all just sort of stirred in a hot skillet. Sound like fried rice? What's new about that, you ask? Well, having it for breakfast, that's what's new. At the last minute, scramble an egg into the mixture. We always cook enough rice to have some for breakfast the next day.

Remember that hot tomato soup idea? Well, stir a couple spoonfuls of leftover rice into the soup before heating. It will keep you going until a delayed lunch.

I guess the bottom line is, if you like to eat it for noon or evening meals, why not give it a try for breakfast? Your stomach cannot tell time, but it sure will let you know if you skip breakfast, and then you will likely eat too much lunch and feel sluggish all day. Even that perennial ladies luncheon favorite, *cottage cheese and fruit platter, makes a very satisfying breakfast.*

Tempting 'Taters

For an almost instant meal in a minute, *bake a potato in the microwave for breakfast.* You can top it with butter, sour cream, yogurt, cottage cheese, sliced raw mushrooms or grated cheese, if fat is no problem. For a change, *try just salt and pepper and a dash of balsamic vinegar.* I kid you not, it is delicious, nutritious and wonderfully low-cal and non-fat.

So stare into the fridge for a few minutes, get into *creative mode,* and start to enjoy breaking your fast. You might just tempt the other breakfast-haters in the family.

For Picnic-Procrastinators

Let me tell you about the day I swore off picnics, until I finally figured out a way to picnic without the hassle.

We were visiting friends out of state. On our first evening in town, my hostess announced that tomorrow we were going on a picnic to a nationally known park and historic attraction. As soon as dinner dishes were washed and put away, she pulled out two huge black iron skillets, about a ton of chicken parts and darn near everything in her pantry.

As she assigned jobs to me, our husbands (both ex-Big Band instrumentalists from way back when) retired to the back porch with a jug of scotch, a recorder and tapes of their favorite musicians.

My teeth gritted and my seether seethed as I boiled, peeled and chopped potatoes for salad; pulled fat and pin feathers from chickens; diced fruit for a gelatin dessert; and listened to the aggravating whir of my friend's mixers and blenders creating homemade mayo, deviled eggs and cookies for six kids, two grown men and two worn-to-a-frazzle women—us!

We had enough food in coolers for an army, when we put away the last mixer and skillet and woke up our husbands to climb the stairs to bed. I fell asleep so fast, I missed my loving hubby's nudge.

Bright and early the next day, we routed out the kids and men; directed their clumsy efforts to pack up the picnic hampers and coolers; shoved waffle and banana sandwiches at them for breakfast and headed out for—fun?

Once at our destination, we had to unpack the champagne glasses—oh yes, stemmed bubblers yet—spread the table cloth, set out the fancy color coordinated picnic dishes and silver, and then round up the gang. Try getting eight males of all ages to sit down at once when there is a museum, an historical site, a fishing lake, boats to rent, a battery of pinball machines and a ragtag softball game in the making... all within spitting distance. As my hostess and I polished off the champagne, I decided if I never heard the word *picnic* again, it would be too darn soon.

Once home again to my laid-back Florida way of doing everything, I felt the world was ready for a few shortcuts when it came to creating the perfect picnic.

What is the perfect picnic?

"A loaf of bread, a jug of wine, and thou...," wrote Omar Kiam.

Now, that was a decent picnic. I've added to Omar's sentiments...

THE PERFECT
HASSLE-FREE PICNIC
by Virginia Elliott

A loaf of bread, a jug of wine,
A wedge of bleu or brie and thou.
But the gods deliver me, please, from frying
foul, packing salads or baking cakes that travel
well.
If I have to share my moveable feast with gnats
and flies, to say nothing of other people's kids,
keep it simple at the least.
Not for me the heavy basket lugged to a site a
dozen miles away. Nor do I yearn for potatoes
drenched in mayonnaise whose time has come.
Give me a brown bag of fresh fruit and a jug
of wine or fresh juice.
Or well-washed lettuce to eat out of hand,
blessed with fresh tomatoes squirting sun-
warmed savory on my eager taste buds.
Save your pickled beets and eggs for family
reunions and keep baked ham for Easter,
please.
Give me a tin of tuna with a fresh lemon to
squeeze, bread and cheese, of course, straight
from the grocery,
A boiled egg in its own container and maybe
a grapefruit, punctured for a straw insertion.
I like my picnics absolutely devoid of exertion.

So I am not a poet. I tell you, any of the above is a very satisfying repast. I know because we did it often while touring in Europe. Everybody picnics there, and they don't work all night and half the day getting it all together. Dieters can omit the bread or the cheese, but not both. A brisk walk in the countryside will burn up any spare calories.

Picnics on the beach or even in the backyard are wonderful ways to keep a bunch of kids happy and out of your hair, but not if mom has to pre-cook, pre-slice, pre-assemble and then try to safely transport a whole menu of time-consuming recipes.

Then there is getting everyone out of the pool or the ocean, then dried off and de-sanded so you can eat all together when mom and dad are ready to unpack and set out the vittles.

Simple Picnic Shortcuts

Try this one on for size. In plastic food boxes, pack sliced cheese, lunch meat, sliced onions, pepper rings, celery and carrot sticks, dried prunes and/or dried apricots, English walnuts and raisins (or use those tiny individual boxes of raisins.) Have a plastic bag of clean lettuce and romaine leaves, and a plastic bag of sliced bread and some crackers. Carry it all to the picnic site in a cooler and a basket.

Use plastic bottles or clean milk cartons, filled with ice cubes and your favorite beverage, as cooling agents in the cooler. Double-duty stuff.

Don't even think of setting it all out. Just let everyone make up their own sandwich and snack plate whenever they get hungry. Relax mom; flirt with dad.

Sans-Bread Sandwiches

One year, one of our kids was on a yeast-free diet for health reasons, and we found that *wrapping sticks of cheese and lunch meat inside romaine or bibb lettuce leaves and fastening with toothpicks* made a school or picnic sandwich that the other kids wanted to trade for. (Lengthwise slices of zucchini can also substitute as bread.)

Another neat picnic menu is to pack *individual* servings of fruit salad, sliced tomatoes, cottage cheese, potato or pasta salad, diced cooked meats, chunks of cheese, bread sticks, crackers or chips, all into half-pound margarine tubs.

Throw in some plastic forks, paper napkins and something to drink and you have a complete, serve-yourself picnic salad bar and no dish washing afterward at home.

TIP: For doing your part in recycling, use paper hot-beverage cups covered with foil or wax paper, anchored with rubber bands, instead of those little plastic tubs.

And then, of course, there is always the Colonel's™ famous chicken buckets or selections from your favorite deli, purchased in quarter- or half-pound containers, one for each person—again, no tiring preparation and no cleanup.

Got the idea? Now let's see what you can come up with in the way of a *hassle-free* moveable feast.

Hey! Here's one: Order one of those humongous doughnut-shaped hoagie sandwiches from the deli. It's a meal in itself, and the only utensil you need is a serrated knife. For plates, just use some paper towels or napkins.

HOW TO BOARD UP YOUR KITCHEN

Be a Guest at Your Own Party

 Reluctant hosts and hostesses usually do love people, but just don't have the time to put on the glitz and plan intricate gourmet party meals. Some are just plain lazy, like me, and are constantly searching for an easy way to do the spectacular, again, like me.

I think the best example of a no-work dinner party was explained to me by an extremely attractive man at the deli counter one late afternoon. He was buying four slabs of bloody rare roast beef, *half an inch thick.* I had to know what kind of Neanderthal would eat such a sandwich.

"Oh, no sandwiches," he grinned. "I'm entertaining and I can't boil water, but I sure can operate a microwave. So I'll just buy some stuffed baked potatoes, from the freezer, nuke these beef slices about 2 minutes and one of my guests is bringing a salad and another is bringing ice cream and cookies. Voilà, a dinner party."

While I was still trying to choose between macaroni and cheese or potato salad, he wandered off muttering aloud from his list, "Horseradish, herring in sour cream, crackers, olives, mixed nuts..."

Now there is a creative, self-sufficient man! I decided to go him one better, so I started inspecting the deli for the possibilities. Let's see now, there was a lovely fruit compote for starters, or ambrosia, and then that mouth-watering Italian antipasto-type mixture. Potato salads, pasta dishes and even a lovely tabuli grain mixture were side-dish choices. There were puddings and gelatins of all flavors and descriptions for dessert.

As for an entreé, well, what could be more elegant than the rare roast beef, barely heated in the microwave. If you wanted to be even fancier, you could open a can of onion soup and slice up half a dozen fresh mushrooms, or even open a little jar of button mushrooms, simmer them in the soup until reduced to about half—presto, au jus! Don't forget a jar of fresh horseradish.

Three Easy Dinners
1

One of my most popular parties is my Italian Buffet. I raid the freezer case at the market, get a large family-size tray of lasagna, one of Noodles Alfredo®, and a couple packages of cocktail meatballs.

Put the pastas directly into square casseroles, (the Corning Ware® items are perfect) dump the meatballs in another casserole and top them with a jar of Prego®, Ragú® or Paul Newman®, take your pick; or better yet a small container of your very own basic tomato sauce from our *3 Tomato 4* cookbook. Make up a huge salad from the fresh, already-cut ingredients salad bar which most markets now have, pick up a loaf of frozen, ready-to-heat garlic bread and you have dinner for about eight hungry people.

Of course, you should enhance the main attraction by decorating the casseroles with parsley or by scattering a handful of grated cheeses over top, or having the cheeses in little bowls to be added by the guests.

As for dessert, a bag of Stella Doro® Anisette cookies and some pineapple sherbet complement the highly-seasoned dinner foods perfectly.

2

Another easy dinner for a crowd is to use baked beans, potato salad, cole slaw and whole barbecued chickens from the deli. Figure each chicken will serve three people, a pound each of the other things will serve four. Put the chickens in a roasting pan, squeeze a little lemon juice. Sprinkle some wine and about a Tablespoon of Butter Buds® over the chickens and pop them in a 350° oven 40 minutes before you want to serve. Call on a male guest to carve, and there you are.

Of course, the presentation is more than half of it, when you are entertaining. Use your pretty china, serving pieces or just be creative with what you have on hand. I often serve an antipasto in large scallop shells during cocktails, heat my frozen Italian dishes in pottery. I am always generous, decorating the plate with parsley and chopped scallions; green pepper rings on salads, and slices of kiwi on desserts.

3

Another successful dinner at my house is fried chicken from the Colonel (KFC® on your side of the pond) and enough packages of frozen noodles alfredo to serve the crowd. Put the frozen alfredo directly into a large bake-and-serve dish, top with the pieces of fried chicken, top the chicken with grated mozzarella and bake in 350° oven for 35 to 40 minutes. Try three bean salad from the deli with this and garlic bread, freezer or tube biscuits.

For a country touch, try deli mashed potatoes and gravy and fried chicken, or barbecued pork loins.

As for dessert, if window shopping the deli case doesn't turn you on, check with the *No-Bake Desserts Section.*

Now, if you love to entertain, and don't mind cooking a little, but still want to be able to be in the middle of the party instead of the kitchen all evening, here are some easy-to-do recipes for 8 or more, including meal plans.

NOTE: In this day and age of fat-, calorie-, fiber- and fitness-consciousness, I am not trying to be your nutrition advisor, since most of us have memorized a million do's and don'ts. Just be aware as you read and use your own good common sense and knowledge.

Menus and Recipes for Lazy Cooks

Linguini and Clam Sauce
(quick & easy, nothin' fancy)

2 cans Progresso® White Clam Sauce

1 pound linguini

Gently simmer the clam sauce only until it is piping hot. Do not boil, it will make the clams as tough as bubble gum.

Cook the linguini to your liking, *al denté* or mushy. If you cook it mushy, don't invite me! Drain the linguini, divide it up in four wide, soup plates. Divide up the sauce, over the linguini. Serve a salad and lots of crusty bread to sop up the sauce. Serves 4 very hungry people. ⟨▭

Now, for when you want to get real fancy for a bunch of guests. The following Linguini and Clam Sauce is very special and will garner raves from your Great Aunt Maria from Sicily.

Fancy Liguini and Clam Sauce

4 cans sauce, remember, I prefer Progresso® White clam sauce

2 lbs. linguini

Three or four extra fat garlic buds, even six—try eight!

One cup nice wide Italian parsley, chopped.

2 flat cans whole clams or chopped clams (if you don't like to chew). Or one of each is good too.

Dump the sauce and the clams and their liquor into a heating container (microwave or stove top). JUST DON'T BOIL—actually stove-top simmer is best.

Sauté the parsley in about a Tablespoon of real good olive oil and grate the garlic buds into it. Mix this all into the clam sauce. DON'T SCORCH THE PARSLEY OR GARLIC, YOU'LL HATE IT.

Boil linguini in your largest pot. Drain, divide between 8 bowls. Divide sauce up over it; serve a big salad with everything but the kitchen sink in it. Place on the table lots of grated parmesan cheese, a shaker of crumbled hot red pepper flakes and plenty of soppin' bread and a bottle of wine (better get 2 bottles). Bow when your guests applaud. ⟜

Fix-Ahead Wonders

This first one is one of those recipes you can pull up any time you need a simple luncheon or light supper waiting in the wings. Enhance with hot bread and bouillon cups of any creamy soup. OR—start with steaming mugs of V-8® Juice. We call that a *Hotsy-Totsy Virgin Mary*!

Chicken Meal In a Gelatin

1 cup clean white grapes

3 cups diced cooked white meat chicken, about ½ inch dice

½ cup finely sliced celery

½ cup sliced pitted black olives

½ cup sliced baby (tiny ones) sweet gherkin pickles

6 or 8 slender green onions, sliced fine

1 20-oz. can pineapple chunks, in natural juice; press juice out thoroughly. Use in liquid required for making the gelatin.

1 8-oz. package Jell-O® Tropical Fruit Flavor.

CAUTION: Do not use fresh pineapple, as it will not allow gelatin to set.

In a large mixing bowl, toss first seven ingredients together. In medium bowl, prepare Tropical Fruit Flavor Jell-O® per directions on package, using the pineapple juice as part of the liquid required. Mix solid ingredients with Jell-O® and pour into oiled mold. I use a 13"x9" glass casserole. Chill at least 8 hours. Unmold on a bed of shredded lettuce. ⌐

Frost the mold with the following dressing:

**Topping for
Chicken
Meal in Gelatin**

Whip together:

1 cup real mayonnaise

3 oz. softened cream cheese

2 Tbsp. fresh lemon or lime juice

1 Tbsp. grated lemon or lime peel

¼ tsp. powdered ginger

Sprinkle frosted mold with one cup salted pepitas or pecans.

Perfect Soup/Stew
for Cool Weather

This is a hearty, waiting meal after work, a day on the links or court, or shopping. I let my crock pot simmer all the vegetables and broth and add the seafood at the last minute while we shower and dress for dinner. My family likes hot cornmeal bread made from an almost instant mix to accompany soup, but crusty

French bread or toasted black pumpernickel are equally great. Here 'tis, try it, it's fit for company.

Seashore Stew

(For a crowd, double or triple the ingredients. The following amounts will fill up 6 to 8.) OPTIONAL: 1 smoked ham hock or a hand full of leftover ham scraps, for a special smoky flavor.

4 cups raw carrots cut in 1-inch chunks

2 small red potatoes for each person. Scrub and remove a strip of peel from each potato.

2 whole, peeled medium white onions per person

2 cups finely chopped celery

2 cups chicken broth, your own, or canned

Put all the above in crock pot to simmer slowly while you're at the office, or away crafting, shopping, or walking the beach. HAVE AVAILABLE:

½ pound sea scallops; ½ pound medium

shrimp, shelled; ½ pound orange roughy; or monk fish; or any solid, mild white fish. Cut into 1 inch chunks. Have ready a can of condensed cream of chicken soup.

When you are almost ready to serve, add the soup and 1 can milk to the vegetables and broth. When smoothly combined and hot, add all the seafood. Continue heating slowly until seafood is hot and cooked, about ten minutes. *Do not overcook the seafood. Stir lots and lots—don't let it stick.*

NOTE: We do not season in the pot. Celery, ham hock and chicken broth are salty, and we pass the pepper at the table. A can of whole Geisha® brand clams, including liquid, added at the last minute can extend the servings. Do not boil them as clams will become tough. ⊂━

Cheese Bread Pudding

(A Great Alternate Starch Dish)

1 cup small dice green pepper

1 cup small dice red pepper

1 cup small dice onions

4 cups 1-inch-dice day old white bread

2 eggs

1½ cup milk

1 level Tbsp. dry ranch-type salad dressing mix

1 level Tbsp. dry Italian salad dressing mix

3 cups shredded mozzarella cheese

Liberally oil a 2-quart glass casserole. Sauté the peppers and onions in non-stick skillet, watching not to scorch.

In large mixing bowl, whip eggs, milk and seasonings. Add sautéed vegetables and chunks of bread and cheese. Mix thoroughly and pour into casserole. Bake at 325° for 45 minutes or until set. Serve at once with any kind of meat and a salad. Will serve 8. ⌐

Lowfat Cheese Bread Pudding

NOTE: I find that using Italian, French or Cuban bread makes a better consistency pudding, whether I make it with lowfat ingredients or regular. These breads are not as squishy, nor do they have the fat content of regular bread.

I buy the loaves unsliced at a bakery and dice them to about a scant ½-inch cube. If I am not in a rush, I use crusts and all and let the bread soften in the milk and egg substitute mixture about half an hour before I assemble the rest of the dish.

Simply use a substitute egg product, such as Egg Beaters®, measuring the equivalent of 3 eggs instead of 2, according to the label, and omit the 2 whole eggs in the basic recipe. Also, substitute 1½ cups skim milk for the regular milk. Use skim-milk mozzarella cheese instead of regular cheese. Proceed as in basic recipe.

If red or yellow peppers are scarce, use canned whole pimentos, but *do* pat them dry with a paper towel before dicing them so as not to have your pudding too runny.

May be baked in a shallow square dish to chill and cut up for appetizers. Decorate each cube with a slice of olive, a tiny shrimp, a bit of ham, or a whole smoky almond. Try a canned smoked oyster or a bit of lox. ⌐

One midnight, while foraging in the fridge, one of my sons and his buddies found some leftover pudding. They sliced up some fresh mushrooms and pepperoni over the top. Then they added some tomato slices and some mozzarella cheese, popped it under the broiler and had what they dubbed "Puddin' Pizza." It was good: I tried it later. So you see, imagination can rescue anything.

This next recipe makes macaroni and cheese elegant enough for guests.

Very Special Macaroni And Cheese

1 lb. elbow macaroni

18 ounces (36-oz. packs) shredded cheddar

1 cup milk

2 tsp. lemon pepper

1 tsp. garlic salt

Enough asparagus and boiled ham (see below).

Spray or butter an oblong 13"x 9" glass casserole. Boil the macaroni according to package instructions, and drain. Be sure to keep it *al denté* as it will have to cook more in the casserole.

In a large mixing bowl, mix the macaroni, the seasonings, half the cheese and all the milk. Pour all into the casserole and smooth out flat.

Now for the special part

Wrap three or four stalks of asparagus, depending on asparagus size, in 2 slices of boiled ham per person. Arrange seam side down on top of the macaroni. Cover with rest of cheese. Bake at 350° for 40 minutes.

The macaroni ingredients will support six to seven ham/asparagus rolls. A salad or just sliced tomatoes makes it a full meal.

The next three recipes are very filling, and will make planning any meal, for family or guests, about as easy as it gets. Either of them can stand alone or be extended with hearty salads and hot breads.

Picanté Pot Ragout
(Serves 6)

NOTE: Boneless chuck, beef or veal shins, may be used.

3 lbs. meat, cut in 2-inch stew chunks

1 package dry onion soup mix

1 cup Quaker Oats® (regular or quick cooking)

cooking oil for browning meat. Be sparing.

1 cup diced green pepper

1 cup chopped fresh parsley

3 or 4 garlic buds, crushed, more if you like

1 scant Tbsp. cominos seeds (cumin)—not powdered

1 can beer (soup can of water may be used if you prefer) or Chianti if papa came from Italy.

1 can condensed tomato soup—*do not dilute*

1 16-oz. jar medium hot Pace Picanté Sauce®

TO SERVE WITH THE ABOVE:
2 cans whole black beans

1 package yellow rice dinner to serve 6

3 cups small dice raw onion, sweet Spanish-type is best

1 pint sour cream

1 pint guacamole (optional) available in deli

In blender or processor, pulverize the oats and onion soup mix to produce a flour. Heat oil in heavy pot, being careful not to burn or scorch. Place the onion soup/oat flour mixture in paper or plastic bag and add meat chunks. Shake well to coat the meat.

Brown the meat chunks in the hot oil, only enough at a time to be able to turn them and brown them evenly, removing to plate while you brown in batches. Add oil as needed to brown well.

When all meat is browned, pour off all remaining fat.

Return meat to pot, add rest of ingredients *except beans and rice, sour cream, guacamole and raw onion.*

Stir together and bring to a simmer. Cook gently about 2 hours, until meat is tender. I do not use a lid, as I want the sauce to thicken slightly as the ingredients cook. Stir as needed to keep from sticking to bottom of pot. Keep burner on simmer so as not to scorch. If you want to speed things up you may cook covered for 1 hour and thicken with the leftover flour soup mixture from the bag you coated the meat in.

Now, cook yellow rice per package directions and arrange in center of large platter. Surround with alternate little piles of black beans and little piles of chopped raw onion. Cover the rice with the Picanté Pot Ragout. Serve guacamole and sour cream on side. NOTE: If your family is not crazy about rice, the Picanté Pot is just as delicious on any pasta or noodle product. It is even wonderful "peasant" fare just using chunks of bakery bread to "sop up." ⟷

Cheddarella Chili Bread

Have oven heated to 400°

Have greased 9" x 9" x 2" pan ready

1½ cups yellow cornmeal

½ cup all purpose flour

1 tsp. baking soda

½ tsp. salt

1 level Tbsp. whole cominos (cumin) seeds *DO NOT* use powdered cominos (cumin)

4 quick dashes Louisiana Hot Sauce (Tabasco®)

1½ cups buttermilk

2 Tbsp. canola oil (or oil of your choice)

2 cups cheddarella or cheddar cheese, shredded
NOTE: You may use any good sharp cheese and/or lowfat types.

2 one-lb. cans chili without beans

Combine first 8 ingredients together in large bowl. Pour into prepared pan. Bake in 400° oven for 20 minutes.

Cover top with the shredded cheese. Return to oven for 5 to 8 minutes. Do not allow to scorch.

Serve cut portions in soup bowl topped with heated canned chili, and any of the following toppings: chopped raw onions, pepitas (sunflower seeds), small dice green peppers. Use any one of these, or all. ⬅

For some reason, men like the following broccoli recipe. Although it appears lengthy, it's a fix-aheader and really is not difficult.

Smoky Broccoli Pasta

½ lb. smoked dried beef slices, from a jar or the deli

Pinch of smoke salt or dash of Wright's Liquid Smoke®

1 Tbsp. dijon mustard

2 Tbsp. lite mayonnaise (NOT salad dressing)

1 Tbsp. mild taco sauce

1 cup very small dice onion

½ cup very small dice fresh celery

1 can Campbell's® Cream of Chicken Soup

½ soup can skim milk. (or water, but milk is richer)

2 10-oz. boxes frozen chopped broccoli cuts

1 lb. thin (angel hair) spaghetti, cooked *al denté*

1 can French fried onion rings

1 bunch fresh clean watercress

With kitchen shears or sharp knife, sliver the dried beef thinly.

Toss beef and smoke seasoning, mustard, mayonnaise, taco sauce, onion, celery, and *one half* the chicken soup (do *not* dilute soup), together in large bowl.

Spray 13" x 9" x 2" casserole with non-stick spray.

Arrange drained, cooked spaghetti in bottom of casserole.

Mix ½ can water or skim milk with the remaining half can soup. Pour over the spaghetti.

Arrange the frozen chopped broccoli over the spaghetti. Pour the seasoned dried beef mixture over the broccoli.

Bake 40 minutes at 350°. Serve with the French fried onions sprinkled over top and generously outline edge of casserole with sprigs of watercress. ⇐⊐

This amount will serve 6 to 8 as a luncheon entrée or as a side dish with barbecue, steaks or roast.

This casserole can be totally assembled, kept overnight in fridge and baked the next day just before serving. If planning a large party weeks ahead, it may be frozen, but I don't think the quality is quite as fresh tasting.

Even my broccoli-haters like this casserole. And it makes a wonderful ladies' luncheon entrée with a fresh fruit compote on the side and crispy popovers or heated rolls from the bakery. The slight smoky flavor complements the other seasonings beautifully.

It is also delicious with fresh broccoli, chopped and blanched before assembling. At my age, I do as much as possible the easy way, preferring to walk on the beach or write a book instead of putting in kitchen time.

Speaking of kitchen time, it's a myth that a man at the grill keeps the woman out of the kitchen. Who scrubs the baking potatoes, husks the corn, plans the dessert, and hands the man all the tools he misplaced and the condiments he left in the back of the fridge?

Individual Cookouts While You Circulate

A truly no-cook party sounds almost impossible when you call it a cookout. But if I can do it, you can.

Provide a regular smorgasbord of salads and starches and desserts, all from the deli. Have steaks, burgers and/or hot dogs—even thick loin lamb chops arranged on a chilled platter. Provide whatever meat your budget can handle and you know your guests will like. Then, the tricky part. Beg, borrow or buy 6-inch wide clay flower pots (try the flea markets). Have a bag of charcoal on hand.

Buy a square of builder's metal mesh hardware cloth and use tin snips to cut it into squares that will cover the tops of the flower pots. Bend down the corners to make a snug-fitted grill. Let each guest build their own fire in a pot and cook their own meat to their liking. What could be easier or more fun? Remember to have pot holders on hand so your guests can hold the flower-pot hitachi if necessary. One clever hostess I know even had her guests bring their own plates, mugs and silver service in a brown bag—no clean up; and, no lost drinks as each person can easily recognize their own mug. If you are a congenial crowd, even martinis taste good in a mug. Then simply rinse your mug at the hose for after-dinner coffee.

NOTE: Be sure to have cans of non-stick spray for use on the metal grids.

Even chicken pieces and pork chops can be prepared this way. Simply pre-cook them in your microwave and grill at the last minute with a choice of sauces.

Even less expensive, tho' it takes a tiny bit of work on your part, is to serve huge baked potatoes instead of deli items and have each person bring their own salad in a disposable container. All you have to do is scrub the potatoes and stick them in the oven an hour before serving time. Have a tub of margarine or butter and a container of sour cream handy.

Having guests contribute to the menu is not at all tacky. When we were kids, everybody brought something to eat to the party, because we all were on meager budgets and that was the only way we could afford to party. Don't you agree that it is time we got back to that good old custom?

One good old-fashioned way to entertain is to serve soup and salad and call it supper instead of dinner. When everything comes out of a can or a freezer box, it is easier than pie. (Let's face it, pie ain't easy! Except for a couple ideas up ahead.)

Everything-But-the Pantry-Shelf Soup

If you save bones, boil them for stock, or if you have some stock frozen in your freezer, use it (See *Bone Bag Meals*). If not, use canned broths; chicken or beef will do, or a combination.

Pantry-Shelf Soup

You should have about *3 quarts of stock in* a huge pot. Put it on a hot burner and add:

1 package of dry onion soup mix

1 package of dried vegetable soup seasonings

1 large can of stewed tomatoes

1 package of dry Italian salad dressing mix

Bring all to a boil and immediately turn the burner to low. Add the following:

1 can cut green beans including liquid

1 can cut wax beans, including liquid

1 can Great Northern® beans including liquid

1 can lima beans, including liquid

1 can kidney beans including liquid

1 can whole kernel corn, including liquid

2 cups frozen hash brown potatoes from a large freezer bag.

NOTE: You may omit potatoes and add a cup of pasta the last ten minutes of cooking, or a half cup rice about 40 minutes before serving, or half a cup barley 30 minutes before serving.

4 large, finely minced garlic buds.

Cook about an hour on low to medium heat until ready to add pasta or rice. Do not boil. Watch it closely so as not to scorch or boil over. ☜

We serve hot red pepper flakes, a cruet of wine vinegar, seasoned croutons and a crusty, hot loaf of bread. A sliced tomato salad and ice cream round out the meal. You may add any kind of chopped leftover meat in the freezer or thinly sliced German sausages or pre-browned chunks of Italian sausages.

Use your prettiest pottery bowls and invite friends over for a "souper"—parties don't come any easier. Put the soup pot on a warming tray flanked by hot breads and bowls. Put the salad on the table with butter, salt and pepper. Guests serve themselves.

HOW TO BOARD UP YOUR KITCHEN

No-Cook /
No-Bake Desserts

In these days of economic belt-tightening, more people are entertaining with dessert and coffee or tea. Some of you hate to cook and have never cottoned to something from the oven if you have to do battle with dough, batters and oven heat. But you can still present a spectacular dessert for an easy dinner party or a "sweet evening" by again relying on your friendly deli.

Quickie Pudding Pie

Purchase a ready-made graham cracker pie crust from the baking aisle. Then choose two kinds of pudding from the deli—vanilla and chocolate are very compatible—or try heavenly hash and fruit salad together. You be the judge. (What! Did I hear someone ask what is *heavenly hash*? My goodness—it is a concoction of either a whipped and frothy gelatin with chopped marshmallows, diced fruit and nuts; or a pudding with marshmallows and fruit and nuts—didn't your grandmother always have it when you went to visit?)

Pile one pudding on top of the other in the crust and chill. Or put the heavenly hash in the crust, chill. At serving time, top each pie slice with fruit salad and instant whipped topping.

Or use a pound cake, or an angel cake instead of pie crust. Just top slices with whatever looks simply scrumptious from the deli case. A dribble of rum or amaretto liquor over the cake is great too.

Try this one. Buy an angel cake, either a loaf or a tube, slice the loaf in half longways, or dig out a tunnel around the tube, stuff it with heavenly hash from the deli.

Open a can of your favorite pie filling, apple, blueberry or cherry (try strawberry/rhubarb for a real treat), and layer it on the angel cake. It is wonderful. Top it with a ready whip, or chocolate cookies blenderized with some salted peanuts. Now that is something else! Come to think of it, remember tin roof sundaes? Well, why not make them at home. Ice cream, chocolate sauce, salted nuts, and whipped topping with a cherry on top.

If you are as busy as I am—get a head start and keep the following on hand in the fridge: shelled pecans, English walnuts, peanuts, almonds, cashews, whatever you *find on sale*. Refrigerate or freeze; nuts go rancid quickly.

Also keep cookies, all kinds of hard cookies, from the *cheapos* in plastic bags to those few left from the bridge party when you splurged at the bakery. Keep them in self-sealed platic bags, either in the freezer or the fridge. *This is why a second fridge is better than a freezer.*

I also keep canned fruit cocktail, crushed and chunk pineapple, sliced peaches, apricots and mandarin oranges in the pantry. A box of raisins, seeded prunes... the ready-to-eat kind in round boxes. Chocolate syrup and chocolate chips should be standing at the ready in the fridge.

Instant pudding mixes and various flavors of gelatin deserts as well as instant whipped toppings, either the refrigerated kind or the ones you mix with milk and whip yourself—all will add to your reputation as a hostess who can do anything at a moment's notice. Keep a box of powdered skim milk on hand to mix with cold water to use instead of milk. This way, if the kids have emptied the milk jug at dinner, you can still be ready for evening guests.

Now, let's assume you also have ice cream in the freezer and maybe even an angel food cake. Or pick one up at the market on your way home.

Wonderful Things With Cake Angel #1

Slice up an angel cake so that you can build a 1" thick "platform" on a pretty platter. If you have a well-stocked bar, stick your fingers over the neck of the rum bottle and dibble-dabble drops of rum over the cake. If yours is a tee-totaler family, no sweat. Take ¼ cup milk, ½ teaspoon vanilla, ½ teaspoon rum flavoring and a Tablespoon of honey — (if someone cleaned out the honey jar, use karo syrup or your favorite jelly—softened in the microwave first). Mix these flavorings up well and dribble over cake.

Next: Multiple Choice.
1. Add chocolate sauce and a whipped topping. Chill and serve.

2. Add sliced strawberries or peaches. Chill and serve.

3. Add crushed pineapple and blueberries. Chill and serve.

4. Add orange sections & flaked coconut.

5. Add chocolate sauce and then run ½ cup any kind of nutmeats and ½ cup cookies through the blender for a second, and sprinkle over chocolate. Chill and serve with or without whipped topping.

Got the idea now? You can also add ice cream to any of the above. ⟜

And here is a real winner.

Wonderful Things With Cake Angel #2

After you have dribbled the cake platform with liquor (or your own seasoning mix) spread half a gallon of softened ice cream over all, then refreeze. Presto—an ice cream pie, which can be eaten as is or embellished at serving time with fruit, topping or nuts. Come on, be creative, invent something on your own. Sliced kiwi and whole raspberries are gorgeous!

If you just must use the oven in order to feel "lovin'" about it all, pile some chocolate peanut butter cups on top of the cake and run the whole thing under the broiler for just a minute or two. Watch it carefully—don't scorch it. This creation will even support birthday candles once it is chilled a bit.

Okay, so much for angels, sweet as they are. Now about those leftover cookies.

Deserts From Leftover Cookies

Using your blender or a plastic bag and a rolling pin, reduce leftover cookies to very coarse crumbs. You should have about A cup. Add with 1 cup of chopped nutmeats and 1 cup of raisins to one package instant pudding mix. Mix with 1¾ cup skim milk, beating briskly with whisk or large meat serving fork until stiff. Chill and serve in wide shallow sherbet glasses. If you want to get fancy about it, top with a huge strawberry, a maraschino cherry, a slice of kiwi and/or whipped topping.

Crushed cookies are wonderful over ice cream, frozen yogurt, and sherbets. And try them over canned fruit or roll a banana in honey that has been spiked with a bit of lemon juice and then in crushed cookie crumbs.

One smart mom I know adds crushed cookies to dry cereal for a breakfast treat.

Tips Worth Remembering

Keep a pound cake in the freezer, because anything you can do with an angel you can do with a pound cake.

Plus, you can toast sliced pound cake and put anything listed above on it, in almost any combination that sounds good to your taste buds...now if that isn't instant desert I'd like to know what is. Pound cake is even good for breakfast...try warming peanut butter in your microwave and spreading it on a slice.

Try mixing a jar of junior baby food apricots with 10-ounce jar of apricot preserve or orange marmalade; use to top the cake or ice cream. Soften preserves or marmalade 40 seconds in the microwave for easy blending.

Living in Florida, I Just Have to Tell You a Thing or Two About Coconut

I don't care if you use a whole, fresh coconut from the market or your backyard, or a bag of flaked coconut. Here is how to make the best puddin' cake in the world.

Coconut Pudding Cake

First, make some coconut milk. There are two ways to come by this delicious stuff.

1. Poke the eyes out of a fresh coconut, drain the milk into a cup. Then put the coconut in a 300° oven for about 20 minutes. It will crack open and you can dig out the meat and grate it. Mix about a cup of grated coconut into the saved milk. Heat and let set about an hour. Strain and save the milk.

2. Heat a cup of milk and add ½ cup grated store bought coconut. Let it set about an hour, mashing it up and stirring it about a lot. Drain into another cup. Presto, coconut milk.

Second, take a pound cake, cut it into two layers.

Put one layer on a platter, poke it full of holes with a cooking fork. Drizzle coconut milk over it 'til it is so moist you wouldn't dare try to lift it off the platter. Sprinkle with flaked coconut and well-drained crushed pineapple (save the juice for another use!). Put second layer of cake on top. Poke it full of holes and repeat the process. Chill for 24 hours. Serve with whipped topping. (Uncle Parley used to dribble Jim Beam® over it when Aunt Clara wasn't looking!)

Note for the Daring

Drizzle layers of cake with melted frozen daiquiri mix, put layers together with instant lemon pudding. Top with pudding, and decorate with kiwi fruit slices. Chill and serve with whipped topping.

Try a tad of any liquor. Just sort of a dribble-drabble here and there. Try kahlúa, drambuie or amaretto. Create!

More ideas—Canned apricots and raspberry jam run through the blender for over ice cream. Frozen yogurt over cake or mixed into instant puddings. Raspberry jam and chocolate chips, blenderized—over anything! Any of these over hot waffles—from the freezer or from scratch. Try any combo over baked apples, or in crepes. I could go on and on.

Daydream your way down the canned fruit and jelly aisles and write your own sweet book.

HOW TO BOARD UP YOUR KITCHEN

When a Meal Has to be Special

 We all have times when we are inclined to put *on the ritz* for a special celebration, important guest or a beloved relative whom we just feel like honoring. This doesn't mean that we are just pulling at the bit to slave all day in the kitchen.

I have a few spectacular menus that really do not keep you overtime in the kitchen. Of course, cook-all-day hot pot stews and pot roasts have been around for years. And we talked about freeze ahead ethnic sauces back a few pages.

For those who are starters, how about perfectly grilled 2" lamb chops that even folks who think they are not fond of lamb will love. You won't have to stand over a smoking grill, trying to time them to perfection. They are not exactly a budget item and you don't want to char them or have them running with blood on the platter. So listen up, here is my never-fail method:

Perfection Lamb Chops

For each person, purchase two 2-inch loin lamb chops, with the tenderloin in them.

Trim off all but the merest thin layer of outside fat and any lump of fat at the tail. Use metal meat pins to fasten any lean bits to the bulk of the chop. Don't waste a morsel.

In a pestle or a bowl, mix and crush the following (these seasoning amounts are for 8 chops —you adjust if preparing more or less):

1 level tsp. hickory salt

1 level tsp. coarse ground black pepper

1 level tsp. crushed dried rosemary

1 level tsp. crushed dried oregano

1 level teaspoon garlic powder (not salt)

With mortar or wooden spoon, macerate until very well crushed and blended.

Mix 2 Tablespoons very fine olive oil and ¼ cup of red wine together and rub all over each chop.

Put the crushed season mixture in a shallow pan and roll the chops around in it to be sure they are coated.

NOW COMES THE WONDERFULLY EASY PART: Spray metal skewers with non-stick spray and skewer the chops on them, about an inch apart. Using one skewer near the large bone and a second one up the middle of the main portion of the meat, place them so they all face the same direction, and so the bone becomes a flat, firm "stand" to hold them up with their tails in the air. Now they look almost like a rack of lamb, which they are. I have cooked 18 of these at a time by using my longest skewers and placing them in my oven broiler pan, not on the pierced rack, just stand them right up in the pan.

Make sure your salad is made ahead of time. A Greek salad is perfect, so is a spinach bowl with mandarin orange sections and sweet onion rings. You decide.

Packaged brown rice pilaf prepared in the microwave per the directions on the brand you purchase is the perfect starch with lamb.

Preheat the oven to 400°. Place pan of chops on middle rack and roast for 15 minutes. Pierce a chop from the middle of the pan. If it is really rare, roast another 5 to 7 minutes. Now you should have nice, faintly pink chops which means they will be at their peak for flavor. Be sure to serve a really good quality mint sauce (you buy it in bottles like Worcestershire®) and instead of the mundane mint jelly, we like a good Major Grey Chutney®. I promise you heretofore, even lamb-haters will beg for the recipe. ⌐

Lamb Substitute

Now if you just don't want to take a chance on lamb or if it is absolutely beyond the budget, use the identical seasoning procedure on an *eye of round*, but use a 375° oven and roast 15 minutes per pound for rare, 20 minutes a pound for medium rare. If you all like your beef well done, forget it. Buy a pot roast, why waste money and a good eye cooking the thing to death?

Let the eye of round sit 15 minutes before you slice it, and then use an extremely sharp knife, slice on the slant, very thin. Meanwhile, deglaze the roasting pan with ½ cup red wine and ½ cup beef bouillon.

Bring to boil and allow to reduce about 5 minutes. Pour over the slices of meat. I find that when I roast 15 minutes per pound, that this hot wine sauce "greys" up the slices enough so that folks who can't stand the sight of rare meat will eat heartily and the meat will remain more tender than if it were roasted longer. Eye of round is touchy. You either have to serve it rare or make a pot roast out of it. What a waste that would be. Forget the mint and chutney accompaniments with beef. Instead, have some horseradish at the ready. ⟨

There now, you have two easy ways to serve up a gourmet production for meat-lovers without having to be at it all day. But my daughter and I each have a favorite company dish that can come right out of the freezer or off the shelf. And you can use up extra fresh tomatoes or canned.

Easy Lasagna (No Pre-Cooking)

TIP: You can start with a pound of browned ground meat, or you can omit the meat...your choice.

Meat (if you say so) browned in skillet

4 to 5 cups sliced, peeled fresh tomatoes

2 cups thin sliced onions, separated into rings

TIP: If no fresh tomatoes are on hand, and you are in a hurry, use a quart jar of spaghetti sauce.

3 cups ricotta or skim milk cottage cheese OR half and half of each:

3 eggs or equivalent in egg substitute

2 Tbsp. dry Italian salad dressing mix

2 Tbsp. garlic powder (not salt) or 5 or 6 crushed fresh garlic buds

½ cup grated parmesan cheese

2 cups grated mozzarella cheese

If you are using meat, toss it with the tomatoes, onions, garlic powder (or garlic) to make a sauce.

In another bowl, mix the ricotta or the cottage cheese or the mixture, whatever you are using, with the eggs and the dry salad dressing mixture, and one half of the parmesan and one half of mozzarella.

Spread a thin layer of tomato onion mixture or the canned sauce on the bottom of 13 x 9 casserole. Then, and this is the time-saving bit, lay raw, yes, I said raw—lasagna noodles in one layer, over the sauce. Then a layer of tomato sauce mixture, layer of cheese mixture, more tomato, layer of lasagna noodles and repeat until casserole is full. Try to have tomato sauce left for on top but if you run out, just slice up four or five more tomatoes over top.

Cook covered with foil for 1 hour at 350°. Those raw noodles will cook in the bubbling sauce. Then uncover and top with remaining half of parmesan and mozzarella. Bake another 15 minutes to melt the cheese, but don't let it get brown and leathery. Lay the foil back over to keep hot and let sit about 15 minutes before serving. ⌑

The beauty of this lasagna is that you do not have to boil and drain the noodles. You can assemble all the rest of the ingredients in bowls the day before, and put the casserole together and pop it in the oven about an hour before dinner time. This is a real time-saver.

My daughter makes a great Greek-type shrimp dish that we all just love. I will first give you her exact recipe as she first made it, which is wonderful. However, she cooks a lot like me and changes things around to fit what is on hand or what looks best at market, so the alternatives will be in parentheses.

Sue's Greek Shrimp

First, you need to decide what to serve with this, so you have it ready. Pasta, rice, split baked potatoes, or just slabs of toasted Italian bread. All are great. Sue usually uses vermicelli.

Sue's Greek Shrimp

2 to 3 lbs. raw large shrimp, peeled, deveined and cut in half. OR small shrimp, scallops, half of each, or strips of chicken breast or Surmi (artificial crab meat)

½ cup lemon juice

¼ cup butter (or margarine)

3 minced garlic cloves

1 cup chopped green onions, tops and all
OR (plain cooking onions will do)

6 large tomatoes, peeled, cut into wedges

1 tsp. dried, crushed oregano (salt and pepper to taste, she goes easy and allows us to add at table.)

1 12-oz. box sliced fresh mushrooms (less or more; you can even omit them if you wish.)

½ cup, more or less, sliced black olives

½ to 1 lb. Feta cheese, according to your taste. We use a lot.

¾ cup dry sherry

Sprinkle the sea food item with lemon juice. (I even use lemon on chicken too and it is good.) Set aside. Melt butter (or margarine) in large skillet or wok. Sauté garlic, onion, mushrooms, black olives and tomatoes together just until onions start to get limp. Add the seafood or the chicken, oregano, salt and pepper and stir and toss while sautéing until the shrimp are pink, (or scallops flaky or chicken white and tender. The Surmi only needs to be hot, it is already cooked.)

Add sherry, bring to a very active simmer, *please do not boil.* Add the Feta cheese, continue to toss and cook about 4 minutes. Serve over rice, pasta—whatever. ⌐→

My husband and his mother like barley with this dish.

Notice too, we do not suggest grated parmesan cheese to go with this. The whole point is to savor the wonderful flavor of the fresh Greek feta cheese in the sherry. I'm here to tell you it is good.

Now this recipe looks long and complicated at first glance. But I have started it about the time folks are midway through the second drink—and since it is a stir-fry type of dish, everybody stands around my kitchen taking deep breaths of the cooking aromas and making me feel like Julia Child.

We also keep shrimp in the freezer, along with boneless chicken breast filets and we always have a basket of tomatoes handy, so it can be rustled up in a hurry. Thank you Susie! She and I both love to entertain, but are pretty busy, so we both try to save time and effort any way we can. And I know you do too.

From Pantry to Platter in a Flash

 Having been brought up in a frugal household, I had more than my share of canned tuna fish. Oh, I know it is full of all the right kinds of nutrition and oils. I really sort of like solid white tuna in water, served icy cold on a bed of crisp lettuce with half a lemon to squeeze over, or in a salad with fresh crisp celery chunks, hard boiled egg quarters and real homemade mayonnaise. However, heated-up canned tuna, white or dark, buried in canned soup and noodles, should *stay buried*—and, I might add—*not in my kitchen*!

When my older kids were young, I was a frugal cook because I had to be, so these two offspring are about as enthusiastic about cooked canned tuna as I. As far as I am concerned, it ranks with french fried Rocky Mountain Oysters. If you don't know what Rocky Mountain Oysters are, don't ask, you'll get sick right now.

But to get on with it, any of the following suggestions for a really quick, nutritious meal can be varied by using canned tuna, if you relish the stuff, instead of or in addition to any meat or seafood ingredient listed.

Also, remember that any frozen ingredient can be used instead of canned, almost, but not quite as quickly.

Instead of traditional recipes with fancy names, I will just list out some of the grocery store items that will combine in a hurry to create a meal. Once you get the hang of it, cruise the aisles of your favorite supermarket and make up your own recipes and menus. These same ideas have been used over the years by my kids when they got out of the dorm and into their first apartment, and now the grandkids are experimenting. However, these grandkids started while yet in the dorm since they are of the age of hot pots, small microwave ovens and dorm-size refrigerators which weren't around when their parents were in college.

One clever lady uses these ideas to package together canned meals in individual grocery bags, with directions printed on the side, for each Sunday collection in her church for the poor. You could do the same as a care package for your college kids, or aged parents.

Meals From Pantry Shelves

Boiled Dinner # 1

1 can green beans, 1 can tiny whole potatoes, 1 can sliced carrots, 1 can corned beef, *not corned beef hash*. Strain and discard the water off the potatoes. Dump potatoes, green beans and carrots with their juices into a hot pot or a microwave dish. (Seasoning tip: add scant teaspoon plain old yellow mustard and 1 level Tablespoon chicken broth seasoning.)

Heat until bubbling, add the corned beef, in as whole a chunk as possible. Continue to heat 'til meat is hot. This will serve 2 hungry people. If a guest drops in, add a can of kidney beans, and/or a can of drained tiny boiled onions. Sop up the juices with chunks of Italian bread, or sub rolls from the corner convenience store. Serve bottled fruit juices instead of coffee or tea; canned or fresh fruit and cookies for dessert. This doesn't exactly call for a bottle of French wine, but you won't go hungry and you'll be out of the kitchen pronto; and it won't break the budget. The same can be said about all of the following suggestions. ⌐

Boiled Dinner # 2

A small, off-the-shelf canned ham, *not the kind that needs refrigeration,* and any combination of canned or frozen vegetables (we especially like the Japanese mixtures). Combine in a pot, bring to bubbling. If using frozen vegetables, use a can of beef or chicken broth for liquid). When bubbling, add ¾ cup instant rice and set off the heat, cover, for five minutes. ⌐

Quick Fricassee: see the *Chapter 15*, about front porches.

Best Ever Corned Beef Hash

This is best if prepared in a skillet, either electric or stove top, but can be done in a microwave shallow casserole. For 2 or 3 people you will need: 1 ten-ounce bag frozen hash brown potatoes, one 5- or 6-ounce bag frozen chopped onions, 1 can corned beef, *NOT HASH.*

Break them all up by banging the bags of frozen stuff on the counter, dump them in the skillet with some melted margarine, stir them around and add the can of corned beef. Stir it around and mix it up with the potatoes and onions. Put a lid on it. Stir it once in awhile 'til they get sort of soft. Then put lid on and keep on medium heat until bottom gets crusty, if using skillet. If using microwave, just watch it and stir until potatoes and onions are cooked. They won't get crusty but will taste good. ⊂━

Sunday Morning Hash

Just before the above mixture is all tender, press with back of tablespoon to make wells for as many people as you are serving and break an egg into each well. Cover and continue to cook on low heat until eggs cook.

If using microwave oven be sure to stab a couple holes in the egg yolks so they don't explode. You can hasten the eggs along by pouring a tablespoon of very hot water over each egg. Or you can scramble the whole darn skillet full with the eggs and call it a *Fritatta.*

Getting Ahead of Those Frantic Days

When you leave the office without enough energy to snap open a napkin on your lap, it is a great gift to have a batch of cooked pasta, any shape or size, or a bowl of leftover rice in the freezer. Any canned or frozen vegetable you like, or one lonely zucchini and an onion; or a couple yellow crooked neck squashes and that half a bag of weary radishes lurking in the crisper. We love sliced sautéed radishes, still a mite crisp, on hamburgers; a handful of pitted ripe olives, a stick or two of celery chopped, a green pepper slivered, good heavens, use it up, whatever it is, before it *dies*. Any of these ingredients chopped and microwaved for about 2 minutes (don't cook to a mush), and tossed with leftover pasta or rice will make a quick meal. Add diced or shredded cheese. I keep a 2-pound bag of shredded mozzarella in the freezer. Need more sauce? Use canned stewed tomatoes, or dice a tomato that is on its way out, or mix up a cup of soup from individual box servings.

Want it to taste like a rich alfredo? Instead of water when you mix the soup, use same amount of skim milk with 2 heaping Tablespoons of dry skim milk powder and a teaspoon of butter buds. Rich creamy taste without the cholesterol.

When we are feeling stuffed to the gills after an indulgent weekend or celebration, we often buy a 20-ounce bag of frozen mixed veggies, poke a hole in the bag and steam them in the microwave for about 8 minutes. Dump them on a platter, toss with butter buds and a squeeze of lemon juice. This is a nutritious meal, sans fats, and if you just have to have something a mite more solid, try a small potato, *not a monster*, mind you, baked in the microwave and don't put anything but salt and pepper and a squeeze of lemon on it. Potatoes have a delicious flavor all their own when you skip the butter and sour cream.

I am a strong advocate of cooking extra. But this is folly if you hide it in the back of the fridge to grow little green fuzzies. An extra baked potato can become hash browns for breakfast. Two boiled or baked potatoes can become home fries for dinner. Three of them can be the base for a potato salad three days later. Two potatoes, peeled and beat up in your processor with an egg and a Tablespoon of cornstarch make four potato pancakes, to gently fry in a non-stick skillet.

Extra pasta, rice or barley, can be added to canned soups. Leftover meat and a can of prepared gravy, heated, can become a hot sandwich. A jar of your favorite sauce can combine with leftover rice or pasta to make a meal. Cooking ahead, means at least one night a week when the meal is a snap.

Those flat 5-ounce cans of cooked chicken in broth are delicious mixed with any kind of soup on the market and added to pastas, rice, barley, potatoes or used as a topping on baked potatoes. For a fast, tasty meal spread the contents of 2 cans of chicken in a casserole and top with 2 individual portions of any creamy pasta from the freezer meals section. Bake in oven or microwave per directions on the box.

Now you invent a new recipe, using leftovers or something from the freezer or pantry. And remember that old dinner menu standby—Hot Roast Beef Sandwich, with mashed potatoes on the side? Well just remember that a slantwise, thick slab of Italian or French bread, toasted, is a great base for any kind of vegetable, heated in any kind of cream soup. Or a jar of marinara sauce and a jar of button mushrooms, drained. Carry home a tossed salad from the supermarket when you pick up the loaf of bread. Using bread saves cooking pasta, rice or potatoes. There is always an unsliced loaf in our freezer.

Try pepitas, capers, sliced olives, cheeses, almonds, cashews, coconut (especially on chicken) thick slice of tomato and buttered crumbs, go on, do something daring to a sandwich and make it a meal.

A Special Word About Seasonings

I will never forget instructions of our priest many years ago when training us housewives to be church school teachers. He said, over and over, "You have to season the peas, don't expect the kids to hang on your every word straight from the catechism—make it fun."

His advice is true of food too, to a point! You will note I am not big on the salt and pepper shakers. Many of my food ideas do not call for any extra seasonings at all. This does not mean that the taste buds in our family have all up and died. But we have found over years of cutting down on salt that the true natural flavor of most foods is delightful.

Also, our exposure to many ethnic cultures as well as the food industry's constant testing and creating of combinations of seasonings opens a world of taste sensations so that if you never bought another box of salt or pepper, you could probably make an old neck tie palatable.

Some of my favorite seasonings are: soy sauce, sweet & sour sauce, the pasty moist chicken and beef concentrates used by restaurants to make broth and for flavoring. (Find it in a squat 16-ounce jar in the soup section of the grocery and keep in fridge after opening.) A quarter to half a cup of any wine will help almost any pot or casserole along.

And I could not live without my dry ranch-type salad dressing mix. I buy it in 26-ounce plastic jugs at my local food warehouse, such as *Sam's*. Rub it on raw chicken, chops or fish, mix into mashed potatoes, into pasta or rice, into pan sauces for a zippy gravy. Rub on buttered biscuits or mix with garlic butter for a hot bread to make staff of lifers swoon.

Lamb will become delectable if marinated with 1 cup wine, red or white, 1/8 tsp smoke salt and 1 rounded Tablespoon of ranch-type dressing mix and a pinch of tarragon. Grill it, roast it, stew it— lovely!

Tomato paste, mixed with a smidgen of orange marmalade and dijon mustard makes leftover meats really tasty. Mix by taste, stop when it is just right. Mix it with any diced leftover meat to perk up a quick stew or ragout. Or omit the mustard and add a couple pinches of curry powder.

Any flavor you enjoy used in its original intent will usually work in a creative way with another main ingredient. The only test should be, do you like it? Remember, some brave cook tossed mandarin oranges, red onion rings, spinach and raw mushrooms together for the first time and now it is famous. When creating, start with a pinch and taste as you go.

Take half an hour to cruise the seasoning, condiment and jelly shelves of your market. Innovate! Forego salt and try new taste sensations. In most cities Cuban and Spanish condiments are as easy to find as catsup. Try them, especially on fresh pork. And if you really want to wake up your saliva glands take a stab at Thai cooking. They have a special way with hot spicy meats served over crisp ice cold shredded lettuce. Most imported products have simple directions on the labels for the timid cook to start with. If you and your family like the trial run, then look for a cookbook of that country's specialties. Most of them are easy to prepare and require the simplest of kitchenware tools. Which reminds me, don't go gadget crazy. *Chapter 16* discusses the gadget trap many of us fall into.

9

Bone Bag Meals

Grandmother taught me to "wear it out, use it up, make it do or do without." Therefore, I never cook bones the first time around.

And, for heaven's sake, I don't let the butcher keep them either. Here's what I mean. Buy those wonderful, thick pork chops with the tenderloin along one side of the bone. Carefully cut the tenderloin out and the main portion of the chop from the bone.It is okay to leave a smidgen of meat on the bone.

Now start two plastic freezer bags, one for bones, one for those delectable tenderloin morsels; cook the larger portion of meat for supper. When you have a bag of bones—pork, beef, chicken, whatever—make a pot of soup. When you have added to your bag of tenderloins until you have enough, thaw them. Then flatten them with the edge of a plate between wax paper sheets, *dredge* them in your favorite "crispy" and have a tender meal (recipes coming up).

How well I remember visiting relatives in Kansas City, Missouri, when street vendors sold breaded pork tenderloins on a bun with hot mustard...well worth the trip out from Ohio!

First-rate pork chops, cut thick, bone in, will cost you about half as much as the tenderloin alone so you are killing two birds with a half-price stone. The bones and soup are free, if you take good care of leftovers.

Speaking of which, we do not pitch a single morsel to the garbage can. Even a spoonful of green beans, 7 or 8 slices of carrot, half a potato, half a cup of pasta, or sauce, one measly little end slice of roast, all go into half-pound margarine tubs and then the freezer. When I have a whole bunch, I combine them with my bag of bones and a can of tomatoes and some fresh onions and there I have soup stock from which I can go Italian, Mexican, Greek, Country or French. I never pitch the tops of celery or their tough root ends. I bag and pop them into the freezer for soup or use the fresh leaves in salad.

NOTICE: If you are dieting, saving for soup makes it easy—every time you are tempted to "waist" a morsel by adding it to your girth, freeze it for soup!

When California or chuck roasts are on sale, buy as much as you can afford to spend, bring it all home...play like a butcher. Cut the bones out, add them to your bone bag. Cut up the meat into roasts and stews. Put some through your processor for the best hamburger a budget can possibly buy.

So you want to splurge one Saturday night on New York strips. Buy them with the bone in, they are a mite cheaper that way, cut the bones off at home, leaving about ½ inch of meat clinging to the sides. You will never miss those few extra ounces of meat since we all eat too much red meat anyway.

When you have enough of these bones to serve about three per person, get them out of freezer, thaw, and then marinate them in real hot, hot barbecue sauce. Bake them until medium rare and tender. Now this, my child, is what Grandma called deviled beef bones. You serve a huge baked potato and a salad, and that's it. Have lots of napkins on hand, this is finger lickin' food. Sometimes I cheat; I just can't wait to store up enough to share with the family and I'll have three or four deviled bones all alone for my lunch.

I even save and freeze the *cooked* bones from large roasts and from roasted chickens and turkeys (if we have not chewed on them) together with scraps of meat from these large entreé items and I add to the soup bag. Ham bones make wonderful bean soup. And of course you know about chicken and noodles. Well, did you know that veal bones can stand in for chicken any time? As expensive as veal is nowadays, it'd better do more than act ritzy in its cloak of picatta sauce!

Here is how my Grandmother got calves to go two rounds, so to speak!

She would buy veal stew meat from the butcher. She'd stew it gently with onions and celery. Then she'd lift out the meat and bones to a platter. She would then cook her homemade noodles in the broth. But the second round was wonderful indeed. She would dredge those chunks of stewed meat in highly seasoned flour and sauté them gently in a big old black iron skillet until they were crispy and brown. With a bit of broth from the noodles added to the skillet, she would make gravy for over mashed potatoes. What a meal...every bit as good as fried chicken, I swear! Sometimes she would make an old hen or a worn-out rooster do double duty too, by giving them the same twice-over treatment. *Boil 'em up first for soup, brown them later for dinner.*

Sometimes the butcher will bone your meat cuts for you and give you the bones, and he shouldn't charge you for the service. A good butcher who wants your business will cooperate, even hacking up large bones into manageable hunks. When whole loins are on sale and are advertised "cut to order free," tell the butcher you want the cut up bones in a freezer wrap.

So, from now on, if you buy meat with bones in it, make them do double-duty for heaven's sake. And if you use them to add nutrition and seasoning to another meal, you have not spent money on "waste."

Let me tell you a funny story about nutrition. My Grandma never wasted a thing. She even carefully washed eggs before cracking them.

I swear, they always broke in half with a nice clean crack. Then egg and shells went into the soup pot on the back of the big old black cook stove to, as she put it, "add stuff for our teeth." Of course, she never ladled out egg shell into any of our soup bowls, and most of my relatives and all of my friends would laugh fit to die when I told them about it.

In those days, we did not have the money for annual trips to the dentist; besides, the nearest one was 40 miles away in Toledo. Well, I grew up and the second time around, I married me a city boy who thought the world would tip if you missed your semiannual trip to the dentist. When his family dentist found out I had managed to live 38-plus years without ever going to a dentist or having a toothache he said, "Well, you must have drank a lot of milk when you were a kid. Your teeth are absolutely perfect."

You know something? I am allergic to milk, tossed my cookies and had to race out back to the outhouse every time I ever tried to drink it when I was a kid. I reckon Grandma knew something important about egg shells, protein, calcium and teeth. What? You don't know what an outhouse is? Ask anybody over sixty who grew up in the country. I bet they will know all about cooking bones too.

Recipe For Pork Tenderloin Morsels

1 cup flour

1 package ranch-type salad dressing mix

1 heaping Tbsp. cornstarch

Mix all together thoroughly. Place in paper bag with pieces of meat and shake vigorously. Shake off excess coating from each piece and sauté gently in a non-stick skillet with very little oil; don't scorch. Use as meat entreé, or in sandwiches. ↤

Pork Tenderloin Stir Fry

Cut up vegetables you want to include, or buy a bag of frozen mixed, using as a base any favorite recipe for stir fry. We use everything we want to get rid of in the crisper and add anything else we fancy.

Cut tenderloin morsels in half and stir fry gently until tender and white inside.

NOTE: You can use the Tenderloin Morsel Coating as on the previous page if you wish. Add vegetables and continue to stir fry until veggies are almost tender; they should be a bit crunchy. ⟨━

We love this without any added seasoning. If you still crave seasoning, add a bit of soy sauce and hot pepper flakes. It is also delicious if you add about 3 Tablespoons of sweet/sour stir fry sauce from the ethnic gourmet section of your market.

A Good Basic Stock

A bag of bones—beef, pork, chicken, veal (clean out the freezer). Use up leftover bits of meat, too. Ham goes well with pork, but not beef, chicken or veal.

2 cups each, small dice carrots, onions, celery

2 Tbsp. beef or chicken bouillon mix

Add water to about 3 inches over the bones, and boil. Skim and add rest of ingredients. Bring to simmer and cook gently 'til meat falls off *dem* bones. Discard bones, strain and freeze broth in 1 lb. margarine containers. Remove fat when ready to use. Bonus: Add 1 can sloppy joe mix to the meat, call in the kids for a free lunch.

HOW TO BOARD UP YOUR KITCHEN

Of Four-Legged Chickens And Rabbit Wings

 A cookbook full of childhood and family anecdotes wouldn't be complete without special Christmas and Easter happenings. Grandma's Christmas butter has become a tradition right down to my own grandchildren. And I never color Easter eggs in the spring without thinking about hunting season in the fall. It will make sense as you read on.

As a child, I usually received a snow white bunny every Easter, to love and care for. Most country children had farm animals as pets.

I was used to eating fat hens and spring chickens, and to the men going hunting in the fall and bringing in wild game for dinner. Though many farm kids raised their Easter bunny for a family dinner in October or November, I could never accept the dreaded thought of eating "Pinky," as I named each rabbit.

Every fall, Pinky "ran away." While I was always sad to lose him, I never doubted that he had just dug out and run off. But one of my older cousins, a pesky boy nicknamed Rusty, because of his iron red hair and freckles, always teased me into wondering if Pinky was in the stew or fricassee.

One November Saturday, when I was about ten years old, I had a nasty cold. Grandma greased me up with her home remedies and tucked me into her feather-tick bed in her bedroom behind the kitchen, to sweat it out.

As I snuggled down, I heard our neighbor-lady come into the kitchen and say, "Here's your wings, Anna Mary. I swear to goodness, when you gonna tell that child the truth?"

Grandma's firm voice answered, "And here's my raspberry preserves. Leah, you're getting the best of the bargain. I only got 24 pints off those brambles this year. As for telling Ginny, I'll be the judge of that."

"Well," the neighbor went on, "My Tom is pretty testy about killing a chicken this week, just to give you wings. He's not partial to chicken, you know."

"Leah, hush. Ginny's in bed with the sniffles. She might hear you. I reckon this will be about the last time. But remember, it'll be your last year to get a jar of my preserves, without you buy 'em at the church bazaar like everyone else!"

I was sneezing and wheezing, and didn't put much sense to the funny conversation. Sounded pretty dumb to me. Grandma's famous preserves were sure worth more than a couple chicken wings.

When I awakened from a short nap, I felt better and went out to join Grandma in the kitchen, where she was flouring chunks of meat and putting them to brown in her big black skillet.

She turned to me, looking stern, and told me to get back into bed. Just then Grandpa came in from the back porch. The two of them looked at each other sort of funny. There was a real *out loud* silence.

Grandpa was putting shells in his hunting jacket. But he paused and said, "Ginny, Love."

My heart skipped. Not one to be real cuddly, Grandpa only said, "Ginny, Love" when he had to give me the dickens or tell me bad news.

"Yes, Grandpa."

He walked to me and put his huge hand over my head, snugly, like a choir cap. "Ginny, I am afraid Pinky has run off again this year. Dug his way right out from under the wires, just like last year."

Tears burned my eyes. Grandma turned from the stove, "Ginny, child, you ought to be getting used to the idea by now. No rabbit will stay penned up forever. Supposin' Grandpa and I would not let you grow up and go away to school?"

I thought a moment. They had always praised my little poems and stories and had promised someday I would go to college and study writing.

"I guess so... but, with hunting season... what if someone gets Pinky."

Grandpa knelt down in front of me. "God made food animals and food plants, just like He made us and the lilac bushes. It's the balance of His world and it can't be changed."

Settled down again in Grandma's big four-poster bed, I sniffled back my tears, closed my eyes and asked God to protect Pinky. Grandma brought me a bowl of hot broth and promised me that if I would just take one more wee nap, I could get up for dinner.

I awoke to the sounds of Uncle Dawson, Aunt Ethyl and the cousins arriving for dinner, which was at noon in those days. The men, even Rusty, were going to go hunting for wild game afterwards. I had figured on making leaf houses in the yard and gathering hickory nuts from our trees beside the wash house with my cousin Mary.

I could hear Rusty calling out for me, "Hey, Nuisance, where are you?" That got me going. I freshened up at the basin and pitcher and thought, just you wait, you brat! Someday I'll get even with you for always calling me "Nuisance!"

As Grandma dished up fricasse into her ironstone tureen, Rusty poked me in the back and said, "Oh boy, Pinky stew, eh Ginny?" I bit my lip.

As the platters and big tureen were passed, Rusty piped up, "Hey, Mary, you can't have two legs." And with that he aimed for his sister's plate with his fork. Even his manners were obnoxious.

"Rusty, stop it! There were four legs in that tureen!" Mary was defending her plate with her own fork.

At that moment, Grandma lifted a wing out of the tureen and put it on Rusty's plate. "Rusty just adores wings; don't you Rusty?" she said, with her eyes grinning.

I looked at the plates around the table. There were two with a leg apiece on them and my cousin Mary's with two legs. Funny thing though, the two legs on her plate were just teensy ones. A four-legged chicken? I wondered.

Suddenly, I recalled the conversation between Grandma and the neighbor lady. When I saw Rusty grimacing at the wing on his plate, I did not know whether to giggle or cry, but I saw a way to get even.

We all knew he hated chicken wings. In those days, you had to eat everything on your plate.

I mustered up a grin and said, "Oh Grandma, give Rusty both wings. We all know how he just loves 'em." I grabbed a biscuit and squished it around on my plate as Rusty gingerly eyed the wings. I just had to stop him from ever making me cry over Pinky again.

I said, "Rusty, use your fingers, that's the only way to eat rabbit wings."

Everyone at the table stopped chatting, and then they all, except Rusty, started to laugh fit to kill.

Uncle Dawson was hugging me and said, "Atta girl, Ginny, you sure got ole Rusty this time."

Amid the laughter, I swallowed the lump in my throat and for once Grandma didn't scold me for not cleaning my plate.

That was the last year I got a rabbit for Easter. The following spring, Grandpa gave me a pony and I named him "Wings." Once in a while I let Rusty ride him, and he never called me "Nuisance" again.

So, let's talk about rabbit. The meat cases in most supermarkets feature domesticated rabbits especially raised for market. They are completely dressed the same as chickens. The meat is white, sweet, not gamey, and has very low fat and cholesterol levels. It takes a bit more cooking time than chicken (unless you're dealing with a young fryer), but it is really delicious and nutritious.

Fried rabbit is every bit as tasty as fried chicken, and will not be as greasy, as the meat is so lean. If you have a spouse or companion who thinks they don't like rabbit, try Grandma's trick, buy a couple chicken wings. You'll make a convert! And dark meat opponents will love the legs as well as the other parts.

Rabbit Fricassee

1 2 to 3-pound domestic rabbit, cut into pieces.

½ cup flour

1 level tsp. salt

¼ tsp. pepper

1 Tbsp. butter or margarine

2 Tbsp. canola oil

Mix the flour, salt and pepper together in a paper or plastic bag.

Wash the rabbit pieces and pat dry. Shake the rabbit up in the bag of flour.

Add the butter or margarine, and the canola oil to a hot skillet. Reduce heat and melt the shortenings. Brown the coated rabbit pieces gently in the hot skillet. Turn frequently, brown evenly, but do not scorch or allow to get dark brown.

Keeping heat low, add:
1 cup warm water

¼ cup minced flat, leaf parsley

¼ tsp. dried marjoram, crushed very fine

¼ tsp. dried oregano leaves, crushed

OPTIONAL: ⅛ tsp. each ground allspice and ground cloves, and a pinch of nutmeg. These spices will give an old-fashioned European flavor, but many folks like their rabbit just savory, and not spicy.

1 tsp. lemon juice or 2 Tbsp. red wine

Continue to simmer the rabbit in these savory ingredients.

When the rabbit is fork tender, lift onto a heated platter. Add one cup of water to the skillet.

Blend 2 Tablespoons water with 1 Table-spoon flour in a small glass jar and shake until smooth. Stir this thickening into the juices in the skillet. Stir until you have a nice smooth thickened gravy. Pour over the rabbit, and serve with mashed potatoes, steamed rice, or any grain or pasta. This will serve 4 people. ⟶

Fried Rabbit

1 rabbit, cut up and ready to cook

½ to ⅔ cup flour

2 tsp. good Hungarian sweet paprika

2 tsp. Aunt Jane's Crazy Salt, or your mix-ture of salt and pepper and a pinch of sum-mer savory.

1 cup of peanut or canola oil. (Peanut oil is very good for deep frying, as it will not smoke over high heat.)

Blend flour and the seasonings in paper or plastic bag. Wash and dry the rabbit.

Shake up the rabbit pieces, 2 or 3 at a time, in the flour mixture, pressing them in your hand to force the flour and seasonings to cling to the rabbit meat. Lay on platter to rest and dry, while you shake up all the pieces.

Heat the shortening in a deep fryer or heavy skillet. Brown rabbit pieces slowly on all sides. Do not allow your oil to become smoking hot, but hot enough to sizzle when you put the rabbit in.

As the rabbit browns, place it on a warm platter to wait while you brown all the pieces. If using a skillet, pour off all but ¼ cup drippings when all the rabbit is browned.

If using a deep fryer, place ¼ cup of the hot oil in a skillet. Add the browned rabbit pieces. Cook covered, slowly until the rabbit is really tender.

Then remove the lid and cook for about 15 minutes more. The rabbit will become crisp again. Put it on the platter.

Add the remaider of the flour mixture you shook the rabbit up in to a glass jar with 1½ cup water in it and shake until smooth. Slowly stir this thickening mixture into the skillet, stir carefully while heating and cooking to deglaze the pan and create a nice rich gravy. ⌒

Now I am fully aware that these recipes are not instant cooking, but the aromas and the taste is so scrumptious, you won't mind doing it once in awhile. Choose a nice cool day, with the scent of fall in the air. Open a bottle of really good red wine. Serve a tongue smacking vinegary cabbage and carrot slaw on the side and hot rhubarb pie from Mrs. Smith's® freezer for dessert. You can do it all the day before, store in fridge in a microwave-safe casserole and re-heat half an hour before dinner. Now you have to admit, that's easy.

Grandma's
Christmas Butter

 In Grandma's house, no child was ever expected to sit at the table and eat a "proper breakfast" on Christmas morning. Starry-eyed children were given complete run of the living room and adjoining parlor with its three main attractions: first, the rosy-eyed, hard-coal stove sending warmth into both rooms from its location by the double doors connecting the two rooms; second, the huge pine Christmas tree, still wafting the fresh aroma of the nearby woods throughout the house; and third, the library table set with Grandma's advanced version of natural foods.

After all packages were opened, dolls kissed, trikes pedaled over adults unwary toes and stockings emptied (remember the golden orange in the toe?), that table became the center of our attention.

The dictionary and family Bible had both been moved to the shelf below and replaced by a basket of Grandmother's hot, crusty homemade bread, her canary glass pitcher filled with foamy milk, an ironstone platter of peeled orange sections, and the star item—the luster glass bowl with a rich mound of Grandma's special Christmas Butter.

All of us cousins had helped pick the strawberries and also raspberries from Grandmother's berry patch for her homemade jam, and had gone nutting in the fall with Grandpa for the hickory nuts, butternuts and walnuts.

By the day before Christmas all the relatives were in-house, and uncles had cracked the stubborn nut shells while aunts and mothers picked the nutmeats for chopping. Grandma did the chopping with her old hand-crank food grinder firmly clamped to one edge of the oak dining room table. She had put up the jam in the summer, and a few days before Christmas she had churned the sweet butter to help bind it all together.

Arising before daybreak on Christmas morning, she had set the dough for the bread. She would be taking the loaves from the oven of the black iron cookstove just as we kids came storming downstairs. Her timing was beautiful. Our stomachs leaped at the aroma of fresh bread.

Today Grandma's Christmas Butter is a part of my family's holiday for our grandchildren. In lieu of all the home-grown ingredients of Grandmother's day, I have worked out a reasonable facsimile, the amount of which should be enough for a large family with some left for gifts.

Plan to make this up a week before Christmas, and be sure to keep it refrigerated—even your little gift jars—because it contains *butter* and you do not want it to turn oily and rancid. It will keep fresh a month or more in the fridge, but I can bet it will be gone before New Year's.

Christmas Butter

1 2-lb. jar crunchy peanut butter, OR better yet, grind your own, getting the kids to shell the peanuts, and take turns at the grinder.

1 lb. walnuts, finely chopped. (English or black will do—whatever you can find in the market).

½ lb. fresh butter, (please, not margarine)

1 lb. pecans, finely chopped

1 lb. plain halvah (sesame seed confection found in deli or ethnic market)

OR 1 lb. *finely ground* almonds
Either is delicious. Both are a bit too much!

1 8-oz. jar honey

1 lb. package dates, finely chopped

1 lb. package figs, finely chopped

1 12-oz. jar of bitter-type orange marmalade. If the bitter is hard to find, use the sweet, but add 1 Tbsp. lemon juice and grated rind of one lemon.

1 28-oz. jar raspberry or strawberry preserves or half jar each. Suit your family's taste—maybe apricot jam?

Dump all the ingredients into a huge bowl. A plastic dish pan works well. With very clean, wet hands mix and mix and mix. Sit down to rest a spell with a glass of sherry while the kids and your husband take turns mixing. Then mix some more. Having everything room temperature makes it easier.

Keep your eye on the "tasters." You want some left.

Pack in decorated jars for gifts or your church bazaar. Save a huge bowl for Christmas morning around the tree. If baking bread is not your bag, try toasted English muffins, popovers or biscuits. There must be the tantalizing aroma of hot bread coming from something!

Grandma's recipe would change from year to year according to what the berry patch and the nutting expeditions had produced, or what the budget would permit from the city market. But the main ingredients, love, imagination and sharing, never changed.

What is your favorite Christmas memory? Does it involve food? Do you have some old family recipes? If not, start your palate to remembering tastes and start your own traditions. Your kids will love you for it.

I Remember When We Gathered to Elect a President

I voted

Tuesday evening, November 6, 1928. Would it be Al Smith or Herbert Hoover? Who would win? My grandparents had intense "discussions" as to the pros and cons of each candidate...

As a matter of fact, I guess everybody in Bloomville, Ohio, during that particular fall expressed opinions, ideas, choices and strong words. Most of the neighbors had a radio of some kind and we had an imposing *Atwater Kent,* which had a drop-down desk-type door like a secretary, behind which three identical dials had to be balanced perfectly so the funny-shaped disk/cone antenna on top could blare forth Amos and Andy, and the news.

As Grandpa fiddled with the dials, his cronies would arrive. They were from around the pickle barrel at Traxler's General Store, the stone quarry where he worked, the granary where we bought our corn meal and flour, and the coal yard where we bought our winter coal. Their wives deposited in our kitchen pies, platters of baloney and cheese, and bowls of cole slaw. I remember one neighbor always brought her heavenly crusty bread, a mite better even than Grandma's. But Mrs. Worley had a newfangled stove with an oven she could regulate. Grandma was still using our big black iron coal and wood burner.

Gram had a huge blue and white granite-ware pot of milk, cream and butter just barely simmering on the back of that big range. Cardboard buckets of oysters were waiting on the swing shelf in the cool cellar, to be added for her famous oyster stew. The cut glass cracker jars, filled with oyster crackers, were moved from the sideboard to the table. Gram's special "election cake" was waiting on the sideboard. (For easy sweets, see my *No-Bake Dessert* chapter.)

With the radio tuned in perfectly, the men gathered around, betting on the outcome. The women settled with some kind of handwork in their laps while they exchanged unique recipes, penny-pinching ideas and child-rearing solutions... really weighty ones, such as when to allow us kids to discard long underwear in the spring and how to keep us from scratching the chicken pox. Girls played jacks or paper dolls and boys played dominoes or checkers.

As the evening wore on and the voices coming from the radio became more and more intense, all chit-chat would stop except for occasional groans or cheers from Republicans (for Hoover) or from Democrats (for Smith).

Pretty soon Grandpa would say, "Can't elect a president on an empty stomach." Grandma would then send me to the cellar for the oysters.

Adults gathered around the big old oak table or the library table in the parlor. We kids sat on the floor around a large square of oil cloth to protect the carpet, and compared our teachers as we crumbled crackers and passed oysters to the bravest eaters.

By 11 o'clock, folks started home amidst good natured slings, slurs and bets on who would be our next President tomorrow morning.

Our election night guests were all a generation younger than Gram and Gramps, who reared me. Most of the kids were allowed to sleep over on pallets strewn around the parlor and dining room. Those younger parents would walk home beneath an autumn moon to enjoy a rare night alone. There were usually several new baby brothers and sisters born the following August!

Real Oyster Stew

(the Calories Be Darned)

1 pint of oysters from your seafood shop. The huge ones for raw feasting are not necessary for stew. So save your money.

2 quarts homogenized milk.

1 pint half-and-half coffee cream.

1 stick of butter (or margarine substitute)

Bring the milk, cream and butter to a simmer, add the oysters and bring back to a simmer. NEVER, NEVER BOIL. ⟜

Seasoning is a delicate matter. Start with just a bit of salt and pepper, taste, try again, taste. And so on. Best to strike a happy mild taste and have plenty of salt and pepper at the table. Some folks like to use white pepper, but I like to see those black tasty flecks floating around stating their case.

The stew is ready to serve when the oysters start to display frilly ruffles around their fat bodies. *Don't stew a minute longer.* Oyster crackers are better than saltines, don't ask me why, they just are, that's all.

NOTE: You can use skim milk, butter buds and margarine if you are really serious about fats and cholesterol.

Now if your crowd are not oyster fans, try my Quick and Easy Creamy Chowder:

Quick and Easy Creamy Chowder

For every 10 persons, open two cans each of:

Cream of potato soup, cream style corn, cream of celery soup, 4 flat cans chopped clams, juice and all. Place in a heavy pot that will hold it all and won't scorch easily. Add 3 cans whole milk and ¼ cup butter or margarine.

Heat gently and stir like crazy. Have fresh ground pepper and sea salt on the table. We like oyster crackers with this too. I find that almost always, even light-eaters, want at least two 8-oz. mugs.Leftovers are even better for lunch the next day, but you really cannot cut down on the basic ingredients for a good chowder.

DISHWASHING TIP: Use disposable hot beverage cups.

COUNTRY BOY TIP: My cousin from Missouri *adds two cups of finely diced ham and a cup each of sautéed diced onions and celery.* Well, it takes all kinds!

Election Cake

Every woman in town had her special recipe for election cake, but as I recall, it was a simple spice cake. Grandma always had a couple jars of her home-canned fruit, ready in a big glass compote to settle the cake down.

Since this is a book about not only sweet memories but sweet leisure time, I would suggest that for dessert you check the *No-Bake Desserts* chapter.

Whether it's an election, a major ball game or celebrating a new year, keep it simple. Even delivered pizza, or Chinese food, or an array of deli platters will serve nicely. Remember, the main ingredients are good friends who are able to share their differences of opinion with good-natured humor and creative descriptions of each others favorite competitors. If your kitchen is all boarded up, make it a carry in. Pot luck is almost always very lucky indeed, with a variety of specialties from your guests. All you need to do is ice the sodas, make the coffee and pile the picnic plates and forks in a pretty basket. It's your house, be a guest for a change.

HOW TO BOARD UP YOUR KITCHEN

An Old Oaken Heart

Where is the heart of your home? The swimming pool? The island in the kitchen with high-back stools around it? The broken down sofa in the family room? Maybe even the fridge at midnight. Wherever, it is usually where all meaningful conversations get their start.

Through eighty years and four generations, our family has laughed and cried; read and written letters; and belabored homework around my Grandma's tiger-grain oak table. We now watch all our grandchildren play on the sturdy claw-and-ball footed pedestal.

This table was not only our dining table, but Gram's work counter. It stood smack in the middle of the big kitchen, the forerunner of today's family room. When the weather canceled out the front porch, Gram shelled peas, peeled potatoes, snapped string beans, and husked corn there. Try it, it beats standing at the sink!

On that table, she punched down bread dough, rolled pie crusts and scattered fresh noodles to dry. I am sure the lovely oak grain is the more beautiful because her busy hands left a patina of love.

After losing their heads to Grandpa's ax, chickens were cleaned on that table on Sunday morning, still warm from being singed over an open burner at the stove. They were plucked, scrubbed with salt and stuffed at the table.

Speaking of hard sturdy tables, I might as well talk to you about cutting boards. *A Science Report of the Agricultural and Consumer Press Service* informs us that after all the flap against wooden cutting boards, they now learn that they are safe after all; better than plastic, says the report. There seems to be something about the wood grain that kills 99.9% of the bacteria within three minutes.

Grandma avoided killing us all with salmonella by scrubbing her table top with salt and vinegar and then with clean, hot water after every separate item of food preparation. So, you emulate her by using a cup of boiling water from your microwave. I tell you this because you will be using an old oak table or a cutting board in this chapter!

Now don't get excited, I am not about to advocate kitchen slavery. But my publisher is the cook in his family and insisted on pasta recipes, featuring *from scratch* pasta dough yet. (What a nudge!)

So, my advice, if you just gotta be a purist, get a pasta machine and of course, a processor to lessen the labor.

Tip to Brand New Cooks

Don't figure on saving time by soaking boxed pasta. It works with dried beans but the time I tried it, as a bride, with macaroni, I ended up with a pot of stuff you could have used to hang wallpaper.

However, I well remember my dear Hungarian neighbor back in Toledo. Rosie taught me to make my first Italian meal. Yes, she was Hungarian, but married to an Italian. Fact is, his folks and he, as a toddler, and her folks, with her on the way, came over on the same boat and went through Ellis Island the same day. Years later they met at a block party and romance reared its gorgeous head. His mom taught her to cook Italian and her mom had made sure she could produce a poppy seed cake and a goulash to make a king swoon. She did her best with me, but the only thing that took root in my head and heart were the Italian foods.

Rosie made fresh homemade noodles every Saturday of her married life to serve with her wonderful sauce—pardon me, she called it gravy. She rolled out that luscious dough with a sawed off broom handle, lots easier than a plain old rolling pin, believe me. But—a pasta machine is easier yet.

So alright, already. Here's Rosie's pasta dough!

I believe in killing two birds with one rolling pin, so you better know up front that this is just about the same recipe as my grandmother's homemade noodles. She used 2 eggs, though, which took more flour.

Rosie's Pasta Dough

1 cup all-purpose flour

OR half whole wheat and half white

½ tsp. salt

1 egg slightly beaten (exception to the rule of no-egg pasta)

2 Tbsp. milk (maybe more)

PROCESSOR METHOD

Use clean, dry work bowl and steel blade. Add the flour, salt and the slightly beaten egg. Process until it resembles coarse cornmeal. With machine still running, slowly drip milk through the feeder tube, and keep processing until a soft ball forms. Dump this dough on a floured board and let rest, covered with an upturned mixing bowl, for about 10 minutes.

ELBOW GREASE METHOD

Dump flour in a heap on pastry board and make a well in center, add salt, egg and milk. Using your hands, pull flour into egg and milk and knead until you have a ball of dough. Dump this dough on a floured board and let rest, covered with an upturned mixing bowl, for about 10 minutes. ⟅━

From here out, pay close attention. If you have a pasta machine, follow directions for your machine for forming noodles.

Poor Rosie, no pasta machine, so she took her sawed-off broom handle and kept rolling, and adding flour or milk as needed to her dough, which she had to hand mix (no processors back then) until the dough was as thin as she could get it. Then she would loosely roll it up like the leaves of a cigar, and slice as thin or as wide as she wanted. Then she spread the resulting noodles out to dry for at least two hours, before boiling to serve with sauces or in soup.

You can also dry these noodles until crispy and store in sealed plastic bags in the fridge for another day. Believe you me, I don't do this often. I much prefer walking the beach, and picking up a batch of fresh pasta at my favorite supermarket. But if the boss's pappy came from Italy, or Pennsylvania Dutch country— naaahh— he'll never know the difference. As a matter of fact, I think I'll convert that broom handle to a tomato stake!

Important Hint: If cooking for a Pennsylvania Dutch buff, *mix 1 scant tsp. baking powder into the flour and dough and cut the dough into 1½ inch diamond-shaped squares and allow to dry and then cook in chicken broth.* It's called *Bot Boi.* That's how *Pot Pie* got it's name. Honest to gosh.

Wouldn't you know it. One of my writer friends with Italian roots says her special family recipe for pasta is better. I think she may be right, so try it.

Liz Violante's Pasta

1 cup bread flour

½ cup semolina flour (Italian grocery stores)

2 eggs, slightly mixed up

½ tsp. salt

1 Tbsp. olive oil

1 Tbsp. water

Put flour, semolina, salt, olive oil, and eggs in processor for 1 to 2 minutes. Add water a teaspoon at a time—may need more or less, depending on humidity. Process until a smooth ball forms. Place dough ball on floured board and allow to rest for 15 minutes. Roll out as thin as possible. Allow to rest for ten more minutes. Then roll into a tube shape and slice into strips. If dough is too stiff for your muscles to roll, simply pinch off small bits of dough and press together to make little round disks. Dry and cook as you would pasta. ⌐━

Now *that* I like! It's sort of an un-stuffed tortellini.

I did promise my show-off publisher some new pasta sauces. So here we go. Again, make one batch do double-duty. Get even for all that dough poundin'.

Garden Harvest Pasta

1 16-ounce bag frozen mixed vegetable cuts, you pick the combination that best suits your family. Steam the vegetable cuts in a wok, or in the microwave until just barely *al denté.*

1 lb. pasta, yours or Mr. Gorgiano's, I don't care.

Toss half the veggies with half the pasta. (talk about easy!)

2 envelopes instant cup of soup, cream of chicken (add only half the boiling water called for).

Mix the soup with the pasta and veggies.

Add:
1 cup shredded mozzarella cheese.

Serve at once with a big bowl of mixed fruit compote for dessert. That's all you need and it will fill up any starving Italian. ⇌

Now about the rest of the extra pasta and veggies. Chill. Save in the fridge for a day or two, very carefully sealed. *To make stick-to-the-ribs salad, toss the pasta and veggies together and add ¼ cup of your favorite Italian vinegar and garlic flavored oil salad dressing (or just garlic-flavored oil and a tad of fresh lime juice).* Serve hot crusty bread with this quick cold dinner for a hot night at the end of a long day. Of course, if your mob has to have meat to live, set one of the men to work at the grill with some steaks or burgers or Italian sausages. This will be company fare before you know it.

Tip for Less-Fat Italian Sausages

Boil the sausages in a couple cans of beer before grilling. They won't take as long to grill, they won't dry out, and the fat will have all gone to the beer belly in the pot instead of on you.

Now for heaven's sake, almost anything edible will go with pasta. So invent something yourself. Just plain pasta cooled, and tossed with chopped fresh tomatoes, green onions and diced mozzarella cheese is yummy. *If there is pasta left over, pile it in a small casserole. Mix up a couple beaten eggs and ¾ cup milk, pour over the pasta and bake at 350° for half an hour for a wonderful lunch.* I keep a couple boxes of the cup-of-soup varieties on hand for great spur-of-the-moment sauces over a batch of pasta.

Quick Seasoning Garlic Tip

For instant fresh garlic flavor on anything, mince as many garlic cloves as you like and bring to a microwave boil in ¼ cup water and 1 Tablespoon of good olive oil. Let stand a few minutes and add to recipe.

Years ago, I had a beau whose claim to fame was his mother's "bastard spaghetti"—her title, not mine! One pot and one colander to wash.

Tomato Soup Spaghetti

1 lb. any shape pasta

1 stick of pure butter

1 can of tomato soup

½ can milk

1 Tablespoon garlic powder (or see my garlic tip)

1 cup grated parmesan cheese

In a pot of boiling water, cook pasta until *al denté.*

Drain and reserve in colander while you heat the butter, tomato soup, milk, and garlic in the same pot you used for pasta. Add the pasta and parmesan, tossing and heating.

Absolutely delicious, but murder on your arteries. However, the lowfat version is good too!

Lowfat Version—Use skim milk, ½ cup light margarine and 1 Tablespoon butter buds instead of butter and milk.

More Ideas For
Pasta Sauces

⌐ 1. Add any cream soup to about 3 cups simmered onions. Pass grated cheddar at table.

⌐ 2. Mix 1 can cream of asparagus soup, and 1 can asparagus, using the asparagus liquid instead of water to dilute soup. Add a pinch of nutmeg, a pinch of curry powder, and top with half a cup of cashew pieces. Serve a waldorf salad with this dish.

⌐ 3. Cook one ten-ounce package sugar snap peas until *al denté*, thaw one ten-ounce package frozen English peas in boiling water, do not cook them. Toss the pods and peas with cooked pasta and then toss with half a stick of margarine. Top with sunflower seeds (pepitas), strips of boiled ham, sliced water chestnuts, or any combo.

⌐ 4. Line a platter with about an inch-layer of shredded iceberg lettuce. Top with hot pasta and then a can of heated chili, without beans, and then top with 2 cups crushed corn chips.

5. Mix about 2 cups leftover cooked pasta with any fresh garden salad ingredients you like, the more the tastier. If the pasta on hand are in long strips, just cut away with kitchen shears right in the bowl before adding salad. Use any salad dressing you like, but do try a can of chilled stewed tomatoes with a dash of olive oil and a squeeze of lemon. Talk about a really good diet item...terrific!

6. Leftover pasta, scrambled into 3 or 4 eggs or a container of egg beaters, and topped with canned mushrooms and pimentos is good for breakfast, lunch or dinner.

7. Got the hang of it? Turn the kids loose, they will come up with some scrumptious ideas.

Quick And Easy Fresh Bread

Now, about fresh bread. Are you one of those people who thinks the aroma of fresh homemade bread will get you brownie points? Well, forget the drudgery.

Buy a *loaf of bread from the bakery, unsliced. Rub all over with melted margarine, sprinkle it very lightly with water. Wrap in brown paper bag. Sprinkle the package with water, put in a 350° oven for 10 minutes*—NOT MICROWAVE—it will get tough. The aroma will say you slaved all day and the bread will taste like heaven. If you haven't an old oak table, just spread a checkered cloth on the table you do have and hum some country music.

The Romantic Weeds of Spring and Summer

 The back cover of a recent country publication featured a photo of a child bringing dandelion bouquets to his mom. My memories go back to school days in the early '30s in Bloomville, Ohio, when we girls were beginning to really see boys—in our sleep, across the classroom, on the playground, and especially after school on the way home—which boy was walking home with which girl?

We would gather a huge lap full of long stemmed dandelion blossoms and, sitting cross-legged under the acorn tree in the playground, make blossom necklaces by linking them together through their hollow stems. If the golden glow reflected on our throat, then our true love loved us. In the fall, when the blossoms turned to delicate silken seeds, we would blow on them, and if one hearty blow sent every single gossamer thread off into the air, our true love would be ours forever.

But the memories that send my taste buds into orbit are about savory greens and wine. In the early spring, Grandma and I would head for the country roads, where village cats and dogs would not have added their personal "flavoring" to the delicate new dandelions beginning to sprout by the wayside.

Carefully slipping the point of a slender knife under the weed, we twisted it around the base under the leaves, so as to be able to dig it out, root and all. By harvesting the root, the green leaves would stay fresh longer.

Back home, we settled in rockers on the front porch with our pan of greens. Sipping fresh lemonade, we would clean our harvest: cut and discard the root from the tender leaves; wash over and over again in a bucket of clean, cool water; then pile high in a stock pot with a ham bone, or some bacon scraps and an onion or two. Next we will gently boil, just over a simmer, for about an hour. Meanwhile, Grandma would stir up a batch of cornbread in her black iron skillet and bake it in the black coal stove oven. No pharmacy can concoct a better spring tonic. Frankly, this is the way I prepare the dandelions available in markets today.

Grandmother often made a salad of the more tender leaves. She might toss them with sour cream and vinegar with lots of pepper...yummy, got your juices going faster than a new love.

Another variation was her wilted salad, and for this, the slightly more mature, green leaves would do—washed clean, piled in a huge bowl, and smothered with the following dressing:

Hot Dressing For Greens Or Potato Salad

4 or 5 strips of bacon, crisply fried and crumbled

OR about half a cup of crisply fried pieces of leftover ham.

Pour off all but about 2 Tablespoons of the fat you fried the bacon or ham in.

Put the bacon or ham aside in a saucer for a minute.

1 cup finely diced onions

1 Tbsp. sugar

Vinegar, as instructed on page 209

Sauté onions in the bacon or ham drippings. Start adding vinegar and pinches of sugar, alternating, tasting as you go. Salt and pepper to taste. Simmer about two minutes.

Now, pour this hot vinegar dressing over the clean dandelion greens and toss like that Spanish mad man. Let sit while you dish up the rest of the dinner, and at the last minute sprinkle the crispy bacon or ham over top.

Let the family serve themselves into soup bowls. They will want some of the dressing to sop their bread into.

NOTE: If you have no access to a nice country road lined with dandelions, you can make these salads with those tasty, vitamin-rich outer, dark green leaves of iceberg lettuce or a head of romaine which has lingered too long in the field. Just wash them to a fare-thee-well, roll up like a cigar and slice into slender strips. Any variety of leaf lettuce will also do. Never discard loose, outer, vitamin-rich leaves.

Variation on a Theme

Sometimes Grandma would *beat up a fresh egg into a cup, add a couple tablespoons of the simmering vinegar to "coddle it" and then briskly stir it back into the simmering skillet of dressing at the last minute.* This was delicious and she often used this same hot dressing on her homemade potato salad. Now, sure, this does take a minute or two in that boarded-up kitchen, but go for it! The applause will be worth it.

And then there was dandelion wine. When the roadsides and country fields were golden with the blooming weeds, we would go and carefully pinch off the blossoms from their stems and take them home to be doused quickly in and out of a bucket of ice cold water.

From there on, the rule was pretty general, but I am sure Grandma had her own private secret because come late fall and winter, her dandelion wine was the talk of the town. I remember the few tastes I managed to snitch from Grandpa's glass tasted like lemonade, but I also remember family talk that warned of the stuff "sneaking up on you."

NOTE: You can make in two half-batches, but compile at the same time. This way, you can use two 16-quart granite or porcelain pots which are easier to handle than a 10-gallon crock when it comes to straining. DO NOT *use aluminum or steel.* USE ONLY *crockery, granite or porcelain.*

Dandelion Wine

2 gallons dandelion blossoms (very clean)

2 gallons boiling water

3 lemons, sliced very thin, seeds removed

2½ lbs. white sugar

3 oranges, sliced very thin, seeds removed

2 cups raisins

2 yeast cakes

Remove and discard stems and greens. Rinse blossoms many times in cold water. Place them in a crock, pour sugar over them and then pour over briskly boiling water.

Stir, cool to lukewarm and then add lemons, oranges, raisins and yeast. Stir like crazy and cover with cheesecloth. Let stand 48 hours.

Strain and let liquid set 5 whole days covered with clean cheese cloth. Strain again and let ferment in warm spot (a sunny window, perhaps). BE ABSOLUTELY SURE FERMENTATION HAS STOPPED, before bottling. You don't want bottles to explode. ⥬

If you don't want to bother with buying bottling equipment, put the wine up in pint mason jars. Grandma did, because Grandpa had all the bottles occupied with his home brew. Do buy new jars with well-fitting, self-sealing rims and tops, don't take a chance on old mayonnaise jars. *Try not to drink any of this wine for six months.* And then hang on to your seat.

Then there was *clover*, that lovely carpet in all shades of lavender, a sweet-as-sugar nibble while cloud counting. Often she would decorate a freshly baked cake with clover or violets, dipped first in slightly whipped egg white and then granulated sugar. Clover was great in salad too.

Do you remember *dock and Lambs' Tongues?* (the weed, silly!) But who remembers how to tell the edible from the dangerous, or how to cook them? If you do, write it up and sell it to *Vegetarian Times*. See, now you're a writer too, ain't it fun!

Other wild beauties were the *elderberry bushes* that crowded along the ditches of country roads. They need wet feet to mature. In spring, they danced with the breeze, swirling their white blossoms like girls in hoop skirts at a May Pole dance. Late summer into fall their deep purple bounty beckoned as we stained our fingers, tongues and lips gathering them for pies, jellies and wine. Often, we would crush a few clusters into our lemonade.

Next time you travel a country road, keep your eye peeled for wild gardens to nourish your soul and tease your palate.

I Want a Front Porch!

 I swear to goodness I don't understand why the architects started moving us off the front porches onto the decks and patios in the backyard. They increased neighborhood crime, is what they did. What robber would dare operate on a street where families are sitting on the front porch of every house on the block? Even with *Neighborhood Watch*, what can you see from the back of the house?

Who in the world would want to hold up in the back patio if you had a front porch all dressed up with white wicker rockers, gliders with splashy print cushions, Boston ferns in white concrete urns, and baskets of crimson geraniums in green or white railing boxes. Front porches say, "Welcome."

When I asked our South Florida architect for a front porch on our new house, he looked at me as if I were senile. I forgave him because he was too young to know about porches, and we reluctantly accepted his fancy deck design for out back.

I want a front porch on a street where everybody else has one too!

I received my first kiss on a squeaky old glider. The spring I turned fourteen, I left my grandparents house to live in Toledo with my mother and her new husband. They decided I was old enough to walk out with a beau or to sit on the porch with him. But, they moved that glider from the opposite end of our porch to a strategic spot directly in front of the bay window of their bedroom.

That darn glider squeaked if you breathed; forget any serious kissing.

They knew when my beau and I returned from band concert and how long we lingered.

Spring, summer and early fall, Mama would rest on the glider between her chores of setting bread to rise, washing clothes, ironing pinafores and shirts and waxing woodwork. (Do you even know where your iron is?)

When Grandpa became too feeble to live alone, he moved into the downstairs bedroom and my folks moved into an upstairs room. Rockers and chairs were moved to the space in front of the window so Grandpa could welcome his passing cronies. They would gather around a low table and he would hold court, through the screen, exchanging wise chatter about how kids, cars, preachers and politics would never be the same again.

Even my friends enjoyed hearing his tales of pioneering, and his exaggerated yarns of outhouse tipping and runaway horses at Halloween.

After one of his graphic descriptions of butchering time in the country, my current beau threw up in the spirea bush and swore off bologna, hot dogs and sausage forever!

On warm summer Sunday evenings we took turns hand-cranking ice cream and pouring lemonade. After the big mid-day roast or tureen of chicken fricassee, a dessert supper was all anyone could eat—sometimes just spicy cookies and homemade milkshakes. Lucky neighbors passing by at the time were invited to sit a spell and share.

Now for cooking Sunday dinner fricassee, there are two ways.

If you're of a mind to, you can buy a stewing hen, keep it boiling and heating up the kitchen all day. Peel a bunch of carrots, half a bushel of potatoes, a peck of onions; and chop a whole bunch of celery; wash and snap a bucket of green beans. Wear out your thumb shelling fresh peas, and keep tasting and adjusting seasonings and skimming off fat until you are sick and tired of the stuff even before dinner.

But why not try it my way?

Easy Fricassee

Buy a whole canned chicken, 1 package each of frozen sliced carrots, peas, cut green beans, chopped raw onions and a bunch of celery.

No buts about it, you will have to start from scratch with the potatoes. So plunge right in and scrub about 8 or 10 little red bliss 'taters.

Using a "church key" (beer can opener, silly), punch two holes in the top of a can of whole chicken and drain the broth into a 4-quart sauce pan with a lid. Boil the potatoes in the broth until not quite tender enough to eat. Add the carrots, cook ten minutes; add the peas, green beans, onions and two ribs of celery chopped about as big as the end of your finger. Cook until all vegetables are just tender. Cut the top off the chicken can with your can opener and put the bird in the pot.

Now for the easy way to adjust seasonings and make a nice velvety gravy at the same time.

Open three envelopes of Campbell's Cup o' Soup® in a small bowl. Add a soup ladle of hot broth and mix it up until smooth and stir into the fricassee.

By now the chicken will have just about fallen off the bones and—voilà—Grandma will never know the difference.

Of course there is an easier way, but we don't like the flavor as much. Use all canned vegetables, including potatoes and small whole onions; fresh celery is all you have to clean and chop. Drain the onions and potatoes, their canned juice is not a fabulous taste!

If your sweet tooth starts nagging while sittin' and rockin' on the porch, forage in the pantry for a bag of sugar cookies and proceed with the next couple of ideas.

Instant Old-Fashioned Spicy Cookies

From a bag of big round sugar cookies, lay them out on a cookie sheet. Spray the tops generously with butter flavored non-stick spray. Sprinkle them lightly with cinnamon, cloves and nutmeg. Use a very light touch!
Now sift some granulated sugar over all and place about 10 inches from broiler heat for 3 minutes. Watch carefully so you don't scorch them. ⟜

Homemade Milkshakes

For some nutritious milk drinks the kids will like, use a blender to add anyone of the following to 8 ounces of fresh ice cold milk:

A peeled banana; seeded orange sections slipped out of their membrane; a peeled peach; an unpeeled pear; an unpeeled apple; any of the plum-type fruits, including nectarines. Also try about 8 or 10 honeydew or cantaloupe balls; half a peeled kiwi fruit and ¼ cup raspberries; half a cup fresh strawberries; half a cup of mandarine orange; a heaping Tablespoon of any favorite jam or jelly.

Of course, adding a scoop of ice cream makes it even better. For dieters, try fruit yogurt blenderized into 8 ounces of orange juice.

Go ahead, be original, what have you got to lose? You could even add a smidgen of rum for grown-ups.

As for front porch ice cream, with all the wonderful flavors available in the supermarkets, you would need to be a glutton for punishment to want to make your own. But if you insist, go buy yourself an electric ice cream maker and follow the directions very carefully. The most important ingredient is a gathered family sharing their week and talking.

When a Gadget is Not a Tool and How to Tell the Difference

 In this day and age, we all have the very latest in state-of-the-art kitchen ranges. Right? What would you do if your stove suddenly dies and it will be at least a month before you can replace it. What if the budget says, never? Well, college students in low cost housing and newlyweds in dire financial straits often have to manage without a decent stove.

Our college son had to face just such a dilemma his first year at the state university. Dorms were impossible for him because he has a medical problem which almost requires he have a private bath with no restrictions on time. The only apartment we found that we could afford had a miserable kitchen and an even worse stove.

What to do? We analyzed his favorite foods and what was needed to prepare them. We found that a small inexpensive *microwave oven, an electric skillet, a hot pot, an automatic coffeemaker* would serve his needs best. Think about it a minute, I bet we all could get by on these four hard-working "tools."

Having undergone extensive hand and finger surgery, he still had the full use of only one hand, his left. And he was really right-handed! Now you just figure that one out. Put one hand behind your back and try putting on socks, tying shoes, peeling onions; or even worse, hard-boiling eggs, chopping garlic or any vegetable for that matter.

We found one of the most useful "gadgets" we could get for him was one of those *mini-processors,* about as big as a grapefruit. This tool can reduce half a small onion, several garlic buds, a handful of nuts, or a couple chunks of pickle to a minced ingredient for salad dressings, ice cream toppings, sandwich spreads, and soups, stews and marinade recipes.

A mini-processor can also beat up an egg for an omelet, combine a couple tablespoons of vinegar and oil and seasonings for enough fresh salad dressing for two hearty salads in a jiffy. It rinses clean under a hot faucet.

A cordless mixing gadget with various beaters, whisk, blade, was also handy for quick drinks and mixing larger amounts of dressings and making dips. We found that setting the bowl on a folded wet paper towel kept it from *walking* across the counter, since his right hand would not function to hold it.

I have arthritic hands and carpal tunnel syndrome (see what I suffer to give you hammock time!) so I can not live without either my itty-bitty chopper nor my big processor.

A gadget becomes a tool when it is something you hardly can do without. But the trick to making any gadget a tool is to keep it where you will use it without having to move fourteen other gadgets first...then having to lift the monster out from under the counter...read directions, and learn all about its capabilities.

Some gadgets we found to be *more trouble* than their keep:

 Sandwich Makers - the various plates, such as waffle, pocket sandwiches and flat grills, required two very dexterous hands to remove, wash and replace. A skillet or griddle and boxed frozen waffles are easier.

 Potato Bakers - why buy, clean and store it if you have a microwave?

 Iced Tea Makers - just something else to store and clean and it uses more ice than the average home kitchen can produce, especially when entertaining. A 2-quart oven-proof glass measuring cup filled with water and 6 tea bags and brought just to a boil in the microwave and allowed to sit for half an hour produces a nice pitcher of tea with enough authority that adding cubes does not dilute the brisk flavor. Use a quarter cup plastic measure to dip and pour into glasses, as the huge container is awkward to lift and pour from.

About a year ago we cleaned cupboards, closets and pantry. At the end of a couple hours we had the back of the station wagon filled with flea market candidate items we had bought in a weak moment. We used many of them for about a week and then stored them away, passing judgement as they are being too much trouble to bother with. As for passing them on to the kids, if you as an old pro find them too much fuss, don't expect them to bother.

Some Goodies Worth Having

Invest in a good **potato peeler:** nothing is more frustrating than one that is too dull to shave butter, or one that hurts your hand to use it.

An extra box of **nylon scrubber** *pads,* and keep one for scrubbing vegetables only. They will wrap around a carrot or potato and make short work of dirt, as well as corn silk.

A good, sharp **pizza cutter:** Try it on pies and large omelets, and to cut sliced bread into cubes or sticks.

Round **spatter screens** for both your small and your large skillets are worth their price in your clean-up time.

Choose a **toaster oven** over the conventional 4-slicer. The oven type will do bagels, sweet rolls, thick breads. It will also set the top of a small omelet you just know you'll dump on the floor if you try to turn it over. Just slide the skillet under the toasting unit for a jiffy.

As for **can openers**, a really good hand type with handles and a turner you can really grip is my choice over the electric ones that take up space on the counter, and always manages to dump the can when you use them.

The simple hand model can be sterilized and put in a dishwasher. Keep it scrupulously clean all the time, for health sake as well as maintaining its usefulness.

In addition to the usual one-egg skillet, 8" sauté pan and large chicken-fryer skillet, I love my deep-sided, *teflon finish wok* with a good sturdy wooden handle. I have had the traditional wok on a burner rim and a fancy electric one. I'll take my twelve dollar stovetop nonstick wok any time.

A wok is not just for Chinese specialties. Choose it carefully. Make sure it has a high-dome lid. An extra wide, sloping shape, steamer plate and height make it perfect to steam four pounds of fresh green beans, 8 to 10 ears of sweet corn, 16 to 20 small red bliss potatoes, three pounds of fresh spinach or four pounds of shrimp, besides being practically spill-proof when you are stir frying around.

I have even made an Irish boiled dinner in mine:

Irish Boiled Dinner

I start a five pound slab of corned beef cooking in the bottom of the wok by covering it with water and cooking gently, lid on, one hour.

Then I add 8 to 10 tiny red bliss potatoes, 8 small carrots and 8 small onions.

When all these are almost tender enough to eat, I insert the steamer plate over them and add about 6 or 8 small wedges of fresh cabbage on top.

If your wok lid will not quite fit tightly over all this, you can simply crimp and seal a sheet of heavy duty foil over top and continue to cook gently about 15 minutes.

My daughter uses her electric wok to keep meatballs hot on the *hors-d'oeuvre* table at a large party; to keep chowder hot at a New Years Open House. She also loosely wraps buns in foil and places them over the steamer plate at big family cookouts.

A craftier friend uses her electric wok to keep hanks of raffia pliable in a warm water soak. And I have passed finger-tip towels, kept hot and moist in my wok, after the peel-and-eat shrimp in their shells have steamed and been devoured. *Now that's a tool!*

Wok Soup

Preheat your wok (or saucepan) melting 1 pat butter or margarine or 1 Tbsp. oil

Add ½ cup, more or less, of any of the following (what's on hand): chopped onions, celery, green pepper, mushrooms, diced leftover potato

1 or 2 handfuls leftover rice or pasta

1 cup, more or less, leftover meat, or seafood

Any leftover veggies lurking in the fridge

Sauté your chosen ingredients together and then add a can of whatever kind of soup from the pantry you want. Stir and blend as you heat until the soup is smoth, not lumpy.

Now add a soup can of whatever liquid seems appropriate—milk, broth, water or tomato juice. The trick is to make it soup, but not so thin you will get complaints about "watered- down soup." ⌐

As I mentioned, my husband is a soup freak. I have learned to never start just a can of soup in a little sauce pan. Might as well set the wok out to begin with; then add whatever is on hand.

TIP: Make him feel pampered, add a dash of sherry or red wine.

It is such fun to toss and brown the meat and veggies in the wok—you'll feel like a chef. The soup may have to set a spell while your family members express their appreciation. When friends drop in unexpectedly, it is fun to turn your planned dinner into wok soup while sharing a bottle of wine together in the kitchen. For some reason, a wok turns on one's imagination. Try it!

Cooking During Power Failures

If we live long enough, it will happen to most of us—you check on the progress of the turkey an hour after putting it in the oven at 325°. Guess what, that oven and that bird are cold, man, cold. It happened to me at 4:00 p.m. on Thanksgiving Day.

There is only one way to rescue it. Take it out of the oven, pull the stuffing out into a buttered casserole, wrap the bird in a huge triple layer of heavy duty foil and put it on your outdoor gas or charcoal grill. I HOPE YOUR GRILL HAS A LID! *If it does not have a lid, make one from a huge sheet of foil, crimping it around the edges of the grill, leaving about two inches of space between this wrap and the wrapped bird.*

Cook on the grill, about *twenty minutes per pound.*

If using a gas grill, set the dial to medium. If using a charcoal grill, rake the hot coals to form a ring around the outer inside edges of the grill kettle, so the bird is not sitting directly over the coals, but rather, is surrounded by the heat.

After the allotted time is up, poke the bird with a long kabob skewer, here and there, and if it seems to be good and tender, tear back the foil, forming a deep dish around the bird and let it brown with the lid down.

Now about that stuffing. Wrap it by the cupful in individual foil packages, treated first with non-stick spray. When the bird is brown, put it on a platter to rest 15 minutes, covered with its roasting foil. Put the packages of stuffing on the grill where the turkey has been; turn the gas dial to low, put the lid down on the grill, and let the stuffing cook while you all wrestle with carving the bird, and making a huge salad. Forget mashed potatoes, sweet potatoes, creamed peas and onions, and all the trimmings that require standing at the hot stove (now out of power). Know something, that was one of our best Thanksgivings ever. We made it fun and were more relaxed and didn't miss any of those cholesterol-filled side dishes. Sure dinner was late, but so what, more time to share family talk and memories.

TIP: If the general power is not off, only your oven has blown a gasket, you can still make the side dishes in electric crock pots and skillets. Also, most towns keep an emergency crew working on major holidays and will send a repairman out to see if it is only the master fuse in the oven that has given up. If so, never fear, he will have one on his truck.

Another time, my oven died on a Sunday afternoon when I was hosting thirty-eight writers and their spouses. I had two broiler pans of chicken parts, all coated with my special barbecue sauce, baking in a 350° oven, *I thought.* When I realized that there were no tantalizing aromas coming from the kitchen, I found that dratted cold oven. Luckily, it was just the oven that had died, not the whole neighborhood power system.

Well, I transferred the chicken pieces to flat microwave-safe casseroles, zapped each one for twenty minutes in the microwave oven and set a couple of the men who were along for the ride (not writers), to browning the chicken on the outdoor grill. The day was saved, and I suspect those men at the grill were delighted not to have to listen to more of our deathless prose.

The balance of the meal was a carry-in pot luck so the hot dishes could be heated in the microwave, and the cold ones were waiting in the fridge.

Having lived here in South Florida for fifty years, I am used to storm-related power failures. It never fails to happen the day after I have stocked both freezers. Fortunately, food in a fully-packed freezer will stay safe for two or three days if you are adamant about monitoring door openings.

However, hurricane Andrew taught us all some *survival techniques*:

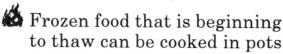 Frozen food that is beginning to thaw can be cooked in pots

and skillets on your outdoor grill.

🔥 A cooler full of bagged ice from the neighborhood convenience store is very helpful, too.

🔥 Stock up on large and small cans of sterno, at least two little, collapsible sterno stoves, in case the rains continue, making cooking out possible.

🔥 A spare bag of charcoal or a full propane tank is important.

🔥 Be sure to save candles all year.

With the world's changing weather patterns, these cautions should apply to all of us. When the "powers that be" (forgive the pun) fail you, don't panic, just improvise and call on your sense of humor and imagination to save the day.

Conclusion

ARE YOU ALL FIRED UP—to invent a bunch of your own special recipes and to cook from scratch in a big fat hurry?

You know "from scratch" doesn't have to involve a million ingredients and hours of shopping and work. You must surely have a jillion of your own ideas on the back burner now. But do try to save yourself time and work in the process, as well as going easy on the budget. If Grandmother's kitchen and my own lazy-day approach to feeding a couple or a mob has turned on your own idea machine, pour us each a cup of tea and meet me at the hammock. Reading cookbooks for fun and then drowsing over some ideas of your own is what *cookin' by the seat of your pants* is all about.

And if that ain't from scratch, tell me what is.

Enjoy your hammock.

Appendix

Table of Comparative Measures

Note

The cups and tablespoons quoted, together with the Metric System, in this book are American Standard, which are slightly smaller in capacity than British Standard cups and spoons. The American and Canadian Standard ½ pint measuring cup has a capacity of 8 fluid ounces; the British Standard Imperial ½ pint measuring cup has a capacity of 10 fluid ounces. The American and Canadian Standard measuring tablespoon measures ¾ fluid ounce; the British Standard tablespoon measures 1 fluid ounce. Three teaspoons are equal to 1 Tablespoon. All measurements refer to LEVEL spoons and cups.

Liquid Measures

Metric	British	American
1 liter	1 ¾ pints	4 ¼ cups or 1 quart 2 ounces
1 demilitre (½ litre)	¾ pint (generous)	2 cups (generous) or 1 pint (generous)
1 decilitre (⅟₁₀ litre)	3-4 ounces	½ cup (scant) or ¼ pint (scant)

Weight

Metric	British and American
1 gram	.035 ounce
28.35 grams	1 ounce
100 grams	3 ½ ounces
114 grams	4 ounces (approx.)
226.78 grams	8 ounces
500 grams	1 pound 1 ½ oz.(approx.)
1 kilogram	2.21 pounds

Approximate Equivalents
for Basic Foods

	French	British	American
Butter	15 grams	½ ounces	1 Tablespoon
	125 grams	4 ounces	½ cup
	500 grams	1 pound (generous)	2 cups
Cheese	500 grams	1 pound (generous)	1 pound (generous)
" (grated parmesan)	100 grams	4 ounces (scant)	1 cup (scant)

	French	British	American
Flour (unsifted, all purpose)	35 grams 70 grams 142 grams 500 grams (generous)	1 $\frac{3}{16}$ ounces 2 $\frac{3}{8}$ ounces 4 ¾ ounces 1 pound	¼ cup ½ cup 1 cup 3 ½ cups
Flour (sifted, all purpose)	32 grams (generous) 60 grams 128 grams	1 ounce 2 $\frac{1}{8}$ ounces 4 ¼ ounces	¼ cup ½ cup 1 cup
Flour (sifted cake and pastry flour)	30 grams 60 grams 120 grams	1 ounce 2 ounces 4 ounces	¼ cup ½ cup 1 cup
Meats Meat (diced)	500 grams 226 grams	1 pound (generous) 8 ounces	1 pound (generous) 1 cup
Sugar (fine granulated) Sugar (powdered) " (confectioner's or icing) Sugar (brown)	5 grams 15 grams 60 grams 240 grams 34 grams 68 grams 140 grams 35 grams 70 grams 140 grams 10 grams 80 grams 160 grams	$\frac{1}{6}$ ounce ½ ounce 2 ounces 8 ounces 1 ounce (generous) 2 $\frac{2}{7}$ ounces 4 $\frac{4}{7}$ ounces 1 ounce (generous) 2 $\frac{2}{7}$ ounces 4 $\frac{4}{7}$ ounces $\frac{1}{3}$ ounce 2 $\frac{2}{3}$ ounces 5 $\frac{1}{3}$ ounces	1 teaspoon 1 Tablespoon ¼ cup 1 cup ¼ cup ½ cup 1 cup ¼ cup ½ cup 1 cup 1 Tablespoon ½ cup 1 cup
Vegetables (fresh) " (dried: lentils or split peas)	500 grams 500 grams	1 pound (generous) 1 pound (generous)	1 pound (generous) 1 pound

Approximate Oven Temperatures

Fahrenheit	Celsius	Standard Gas	Regulo
250°F	121.1	¼	5
300°F	148.9	1	6
350°F	176.7	4	7
400°F	204.4	6	8
450°F	232.2	8	9

Emergency Substitutions

An emergency is the only excuse for using a substitute ingredient—recipe results will vary. Following are some stand-ins for staples.

For	Use
1 ½ teaspoons cornstarch	1 Tablespoon flour
1 whole egg	2 egg yolks plus 1 Tablespoon water (in cookies) or 2 egg yolks (in custards and similar mixtures)
1 cup fresh whole milk	½ cup evaporated milk plus ½ cup water or 1 cup reconstituted non-fat dry milk plus 2 Tablespoons butter

1 ounce unsweetened chocolate	3 Tablespoons cocoa plus 1 Tablespoon fat
1 cup honey	¼ cups sugar plus ¼ cup liquid

Equivalent Measures

Pinch or dash	= less than ⅛ teaspoon
3 teaspoons	= 1 Tablespoon
2 Tablespoons	= 1 fluid ounce
1 jigger	= 1 ½ fluid ounce
4 Tablespoons	= ¼ cup
5 Tablespoons + 1 teaspoon	= ⅓ cup
8 Tablespoons	= ½ cup
10 Tablespoons + 2 teaspoons	= ⅔ cup
12 Tablespoons	= ¾ cup
16 Tablespoons	= 1 cup
1 cup	= 8 fluid ounces
2 cups	= 1 pint
2 pints	= 1 quart
⅘ quarts	= 25.5 fluid ounces
1 quart	= 32 fluid ounces
4 quarts	= 1 gallon
2 gallons (dry measure)	= 1 peck
4 pecks	= 1 bushel

Glossary

Al denté- cooked just enough to retain a somewhat firm texture.

Braise- brown in a small amount of oil, in a heavy pot, until lightly brown, then add liquid paringly as ingredients cook until done. Stew meats are usually started off this way and then cooked slowly with the rest of the ingredients.

Casserole- crockery or glass dish or metal pot that is oven microwavable. If made of metal, top-of-stove proof, in which a recipe can be started, cooked and served.

Dredge- to press an article of food, usually meat, into a "crisping medium," such as seasoned flour, fine cracker or bread crumbs or crushed cereals, before frying or oven roasting, so as to obtain a crisp outer crust. This can also be accomplished by shaking the meat or vegetable in a paper or plastic bag with the seasoned crumbs or flour.

Macerate- to crush and mix with a liquid ingredient such as juice or oil or butter, to create a seasoning agent that can then be rubbed on meat or vegetable before cooking. This was the original use for a mortar and pestle. Chefs often do this with garlic buds and a teaspoon of oil, on a cutting board, with the back of a chef's knife; by mincing and mashing and pulling together and mashing over several times.

Marinade- a mixture of liquid and spice ingredients in which to marinate (soak) meats to tenderize and to increase flavor.

Oven Fry- dredge in a coating, roast in oven to obtain a crisp item without the use of oil as in frying. The pieces should be about an inch apart and turned over halfway through cooking time.

Reduce- vigorously boil a liquid until reduced about half, resulting in a rich tasting base for a sauce or gravy. When adding wine to a liquid ingredient, the flavor remains, but the alcohol content cooks away.

Sauté- to fry very lightly, in a small amount of oil or liquid, such as broth, so as to partially cook and to lightly brown; some chefs now call this "sweating the ingredient."

Sear- place in hot skillet to fast brown on high heat to seal in juices. Must be watched closely to prevent scorching.

Stir Fry- tossed and turned constantly while cooking to *al dente* stage, in hardly any oil or liquid, usually in a hot skillet or wok. Watch constantly to prevent scorching.

Tenderize- to flatten meats with a mallet or side of a heavy saucer. Sometimes, as in case of flank steak, this can be accomplished by criss-crossing cuts with sharp knife only about one quarter of the way through the item, on both sides. Marinating can also tenderize center cuts of economy meats.

About the Author

Ginny Elliott has been involved with food, family and folks all her life. She was reared by her grandparents in a small northwestern Ohio town, Bloomville. Her family grew everything they ate except for sugar, flour, spices, beef and milk. Although money was scarce, food was carried home to the city with relatives, and to neighbors in crisis and in celebration: As a bride in the late 1930's, the Depression called for Grandma's rules to be Ginny's guidelines: *Use it up, wear it our, make it do or do without.*

When homemaking or "Homing" as Ginny calls it (after all, a nurse is nursing, isn't she?), got to be a bit of a bore she got involved in her community. She produced a PTA program about family dilemmas which led to public speaking and a television call-in talk show.

With the break-up of her marriage, she became a single mother in need of a salary. Instead of hoping every thirteen weeks her TV show would be sold, Ginny went staff instead of talent.

One day while working as a department secretary for WFTL TV, Ft. Lauderdale, Florida, the hostess of the cooking show failed to arrive. The show's director had been the director on Ginny's three shows. He had no fill-in film ready and asked Ginny to take over. They both ran the risk of loosing their jobs. (Storer Broadcasting Rule #1, you are either staff or talent, never both. And Rule #2, always have a backup film at the ready.) The lure of the little red camera lights called to her. It was five minutes to air time. She sent the janitor across the street to a hotel kitchen for a loaf of bread and a "couple hand fulls of whatever ground meat they had on hand."

When the red lights came on, Ginny started chatting with the viewers about how to make a pudding cake with local coconuts. (See *Chapter 6* of this book.) With the bread and half a pound of sausage she created some canapés. It was a success. The two culprits were not fired and Ginny was a future guest on the show many times.

When a second marriage plunged her back into *homing*, with a new family and putting on corporate dinner parties for her new husband and his clients, the idea of doing a cookbook was born...but simmered away on the back burner. Finally, when requests for recipes from guests could be ignored no longer, Ginny sat down at the computer.

Ginny now lives in Naples, Florida, with her family. Her articles have appeared in *The Naples Star, Home and Condo, Neapolitan Magazine, Naples Now, Naples Daily News, Golf Week Magazine.* She has won prizes for her recipes in *Better Homes and Gardens, The Great American Dessert Book,* and she contributes regularly to local market and consumer papers.

Today, two career families and single parents are trying to nurture each other and children while stretching their horizons and their dollars. Again, Grandma's values fall into place along side budget foods, and convenience techniques. Ginny says, "I have always had more in mind to do than there was time, so my golden rule in the kitchen is: It has to be easy and quick, delicious enough to get me applause, healthful enough to please my doctor and frugal enough to keep Grandma from haunting me."

Index

S

THREE TOMATO FOUR
How to Pick, Cook and Eat Tomatoes

A delightful and practical little book packed with the world's most delicious tomato-based recipes. All these mouth-watering dishes are developed and prepared with love by Master Cook Virginia Elliott.

You will learn:
* The secrets to choosing the right tomatoes.
* How to store your big berries.
* How to make the world's best spaghetti sauce (it's so easy).
* And of course, how to make those famous fried green tomatoes.
* And much, much more...

      If you hate tomatoes, don't buy this book... you might start enjoying them, and who knows what could happen next! If you love tomatoes, *you need* these luscious recipes. If you don't have enough money to buy *THREE TOMATO FOUR,* send your best *working* watch in exchange for this book being sent to you. Believe us, you would rather have this little primer than know the time of day anyway.

64 pages $6.00, includes shipping and handling.

THE SCIENCE OF WELL-BEING

      The Science of Well-Being encompasses the what, when, where, how and why of practical scientific healthy habits, with suggestions on eating, drinking, sleeping, breathing and exercising. You can enjoy perfect physical and mental health by following these common sense formulas... a guidebook with an easy-to-follow and reasonable program for health!

      Authors of the best-sellers, *The Science of Getting Rich* and *The Science of Becoming Excellent,* Wattles and Powell have completed their trilogy. By applying theory to functionality, they take a back-to-basics and pragmatical approach to YOUR greater Health, Wealth and Happiness!

ISBN 1-56087-059-1, quality paperback, $8.95 and $3.50 s/h Write, Phone or Fax for FREE catalog.